THE HISTORY OF THE
MORMONS
IN
ARGENTINA

THE HISTORY OF THE MORMONS IN ARGENTINA

Nestor Curbelo

Translated by Erin B. Jennings

GREG KOFFORD BOOKS
SALT LAKE CITY, 2009

Copyright © 2009 Greg Kofford Books, Inc.
Original Spanish edition copyright © 2000 Nestor Curbelo.
Cover design copyright © 2009 Greg Kofford Books, Inc.
Cover design by John Hamer
Print-On-Demand printing, 2018
Published in the USA.

All rights reserved. No part of this volume may be reproduced in any form without written permission from the publisher, Greg Kofford Books. The views expressed herein are the responsibility of the author and do not necessarily represent the position of Greg Kofford Books.

Paperback ISBN: 978-1-58958-052-7
Also available in ebook.

Greg Kofford Books
P.O. Box 1362
Draper, UT 84020
www.gregkofford.com
facebook.com/gkbooks
twitter.com/gkbooks

Library of Congress Cataloging-in-Publication Data

Curbelo, Nestor, 1952-
[Historia de los Mormones en Argentina. English]
The history of the Mormons in Argentina / by Nestor Curbelo ; translated by Erin B. Jennings. -- 1st English ed.   p. cm.

Includes bibliographical references and index.
ISBN 1-58958-051-6 (limited edition leather : alk. paper)
ISBN 1-58958-052-4 (softcover : alk. paper)

1. Church of Jesus Christ of Latter-day Saints--Argentina--History.
2. Argentina--Church history. I. Title.
BX8617.A7C87 2004
289.3'82--dc22

2004000182

CONTENTS

ILLUSTRATIONS xxv

INTRODUCTION xxix
A History of Faith xxx
Before Arriving in Argentina xxx

Chapter 1
THE PACIFIC MISSION 1
The Trip to Chile 3
The Death of Omner Pratt 5
A Month in Quillota 7
The Return to California 8
An Apostle's Vision 9
The Situation in Chile in 1851 10

Chapter 2
BEGINNING THE WORK IN MEXICO 13
Looking at South America 17
The Translation of the Book of Mormon into Spanish 18
The Conversion of Melíton González Trejo 18
The Translation of the Doctrine and Covenants
   and the Pearl of Great Price 25

Contents

Chapter 3
THE SOUTH AMERICA MISSION 31
The Missionaries Arrive in South America 32
The First Converts in South America 33
The Dedication of South America 36
The Second Group of Missionaries 38
Elder Melvin J. Ballard 39
The Gianfelice Family 42
The Presidency of Reinhold Stoof (1926–35) 45
The Gospel and the Lamanites 47
The Visit of Elder J. Reuben Clark 52
The Mission of Reinhold Stoof Ends 52
The Church in Rosario 52
The First Baptisms 53

Chapter 4
THE BRAZIL AND ARGENTINA MISSIONS 57
The Church in Brazil 58
The Argentina Mission 59
The Presidency of W. Ernest Young (1935–38) 59
The Presidency of Frederick S. Williams (1938–42) 60
The Williams Family, Pioneers of South America 63
The First Chapel in Argentina 67
The First Argentina Missionaries 70
The Presidency of James L. Barker (1942–44) 76
The Second Presidency of W. Ernest Young (1944–49) 77
Memories of That Time 77
Fermín Barjollo 78
The Visit of Elder Stephen L Richards 82

Contents

Chapter 5
A CHURCH OF IMMIGRANTS 87
The Avila Family 87
The Dömrose Family 93
The Welsh Saints of Patagonia 96
The Church in Córdoba 100
The Pioneers 100
Thomas M. Looney, Pioneer of Bahía Blanca 103
The First Missionaries in Mendoza 107

Chapter 6
FOUNDATIONS OF LOCAL LEADERSHIP 111
The Presidency of Harold Brown (1949–52) 111
Juan Carlos Avila 112
The Visit of President David O. McKay 115
The Meeting with Juan D. Perón 117

Chapter 7
THE GREAT MISSIONS 123
The Church in Salta 126
The Church in Tucumán 128
The Church in Resistencia 131

Chapter 8
THE GOSPEL REACHES ALL OF SOUTH AMERICA 135
The Expansion of the Gospel in South America 135
The Mountain Range Mission 137

Contents

Chapter 9
THE FIRST STAKES 143
The Organization of the Buenos Aires Stake 145
Other Stakes 147
Travels to Salt Lake City 149

Chapter 10
THE MISSION PRESIDENTS 153
The Presidents of the Argentina Mission 154
The Local Presidents of the Mission 158
Argentine Men Who Served As Mission Presidents 159

Chapter 11
BEFORE THE TEMPLES 161
The Temple Ordinances in Spanish 164
The Genealogical Registries 165

Chapter 12
SÃO PAULO, FIRST TEMPLE IN SOUTH AMERICA 169

Chapter 13
THE BUENOS AIRES TEMPLE 175
The Dedication of the Buenos Aires Temple 178
The Dedicatory Prayer 180

Chapter 14
THE AREA PRESIDENCIES 189
The Presidency of the South America South Area 191
Instituting Area Presidencies 194

Chapter 15
THE CHALLENGE OF SELF–SUFFICIENCY   199
Elder Angel Abrea   201
"One of the Strongest in the Kingdom"   202

Chapter 16
A NEW CENTURY   209

Appendix A
HISTORICAL TIMELINE   217
Part I—Background 1844–1922   217
Part II—The Missions in South America 1923–65   219
Part III—The Stakes of Zion 1966–77   222
Part IV—Temples 1978–84   224
Part V—Watching the Future 1985–2002   224

Appendix B
Oral Histories   231

BIBLIOGRAPHY   235

INDEX   241

CHRONOLOGY

1844	June 27	Joseph and Hyrum Smith are martyred in Carthage, Illinois.
1845	Sept. 9	Church elders declare their intention to move the Church west.
1846	Feb. 4	The Saints begin to leave Nauvoo. The Brooklyn sails from New York City with a company of 238 Saints en route to San Francisco, California.
	May 1	Dedication of the Nauvoo Temple
	July 29	The Brooklyn reaches San Francisco.
	Sept. 17	The last group of Saints leaves Nauvoo.
1847	July 22	The vanguard company of pioneers reach the Valley of the Great Salt Lake.
	July 28	Brigham Young designates the site of the Salt Lake Temple.
1850-04		Missions of the Church are organized in Scandinavia, France, Italy, Switzerland, Hawaii, India, Malta, Gibraltar, Germany, South Africa, and the islands of the Pacific.

History of the Mormons in Argentina

1851	Sept. 5	Apostle Parley P. Pratt, president of the South American and South Pacific mission, his pregnant wife, Phoebe Sopher Pratt, and Elder Rufus S. Allen sail for Chile.
	Nov. 8	The missionaries arrive in Valparíso.
	Nov. 30	Phoebe S. Pratt gives birth to son Omner who dies Jan. 7, 1852
1852	Jan. 25	The missionaries go to Quillota, Chile.
	March 2	The missionaries return to Valparíso, leave Chile, and return to California.
1867		The construction of the Salt Lake Temple and the tabernacle are finalized.
1869		The transcontinental railroad is completed, with the eastern and western segments meeting at Promontory Point, Utah.
1876		In Salt Lake City, Melíton Gonzalez Trejo is baptized and begins to translate the Book of Mormon into Spanish.
	Jan. 7	The first missionaries enter Mexico.
1877	Aug. 29	President Brigham Young dies and is succeeded by John Taylor, president of the Quorum of the Twelve.
1886		The first Spanish edition of the Book of Mormon is published.
1893	April 6	President Woodruff dedicates the Salt Lake Temple.

1898	Sep. 2	Wilfred Woodruff dies and is succeeded by Lorenzo Snow.
1912		The Seminary program, weekday religious instruction for LDS youth, begins in Salt Lake City.
1923		Andrew Jenson, assistant Church historian, and Thomas S. Page visit South America.
1925	Sept. 4	The First Presidency call Elder Melvin J. Ballard to the South America Mission.
	Oct. 8	The First Presidency set apart Elders Melvin J. Ballard, Rulon S. Wells, and Rey L. Pratt as South American missionaries.
	Dec. 25	Elder Ballard dedicates South America for the preaching of the gospel.
1926	Jan. 4	Elder Wells becomes ill and returns to the United States. The missionaries in Buenos Aires rent Rivadavia 8972, the Church's first meeting hall/mission home. The first baptism is that of Eladia Cifuentes of Argentina.
	June 6	The second president of the South America Mission, Reinhold Stoof, and his wife, Ella, arrive in Buenos Aires.
	July 23	Elders Ballard and Pratt return to the United States.
1927	Sept. 10	Mission headquarters moves to Habana 3330 in Buenos Aires.

xiv   History of the Mormons in Argentina

1930	Nov. 13	President Stoof, Elder Victor T. Wheeler, and Elder Lothaire A. Bluth travel to Rosario, Argentina, and rent a meeting hall at San Juan 3548.
1933	Dec. 28	President J. Reuben Clark visits Montevideo and attends the Liniers Branch in Buenos Aires.
1935		The South America Mission is divided, creating the Brazil and Argentina missions.
	Aug. 22	The Stoof family returns to the United States. W. Ernest Young presides over the Argentina Mission.
	Dec. 28	La Plata, Argentina, is opened for missionary work.
1936	April	The Welfare Plan is introduced at April general conference.
1938	Aug. 22	Frederick S. Williams is called as president of the Argentina Mission to replace W. Ernest Young.
1939	Feb. 9	The Liniers Chapel at the corner of Tolerno and Cañada de Gómez is dedicated. Luis Constantini, the first missionary from Argentina, is called.
1942	Aug. 1	James Barker replaced Frederick S. Williams as president of the Argentina Mission.

1944	June 25	The Montevideo Branch is organized.
	Sept.	W. Ernest Young returns to preside over the Argentina Mission for the second time.
1945	May 14	President Heber J. Grant dies and is succeeded by George Albert Smith.
1946		New missionaries are sent to Argentina after World War II ends.
1947		The Uruguay Mission is organized with Frederick S. Williams as president. W. Ernest Young is president of the Argentina Mission.
1948	Feb. 3	Elder Stephen L Richards of the Quorum of the Twelve visits the Argentina Mission.
	Feb. 27	The Argentina Mission home is moved to Virrey del Pino 2130, Belgrano, Buenos Aires.
1949		Harold Brown replaces W. Ernest Young as president of the Argentina Mission.
1951		Upon the death of President George Albert Smith, David O. McKay becomes Church president.
1952		Lee B. Valentine replaces Harold Brown as president of the Argentina Mission.

1954	Jan. 2	President McKay visits Europe, South Africa, South America, and Central America, the first Church president to come to South America.
	Feb. 1	President McKay travels to Buenos Aires.
	Feb. 3	President McKay pays a call on Juan D. Perón, president of Argentina. He visits the Saints in Rosario.
	Feb. 7	A conference is held in the Teatro Nacional Cervantes.
	Feb. 8	President McKay visits Santiago, Chile.
1955	April	The mission publication *El Mesajero Deseret* is replaced by the *Liahona*.
	June	President Lee B. Valentine opens missionary work in Santiago.
	Dec. 30	The first LDS Church meeting is held in La Plata, Chile.
1956	Aug. 29	President Lorin N. Pace replaces Lee B. Valentine as president of the Argentina Mission.
1959	Jan. 21	Elder Spencer W. Kimball visits the Argentina Mission and creates the Andes Mission, with headquarters in Santiago, Chile. Vernon Sharp becomes its first president.
1960		The building missionary program is established in areas where members need chapels.
	Oct. 21	The first Directive Council of the Argentina Mission is organized.

(1960)		C. Laird Snelgrove replaces Lorin N. Pace as president of the Argentina Mission.
	Nov. 15	President Joseph Fielding Smith visits the Argentina Mission, accompanied by Elder A. Theodore Tuttle.
1961		Elder Tuttle becomes mission director of South America.
	April	The Caseros Chapel is completed.
1962	Sept. 16	The North Argentina Mission is organized with Ronald V. Stone as president.
1963	Jan.	Elder Hugh B. Brown visits the Saints in Argentina. Arthur Strong replaces C. Laird Snelgrove as president of the Argentina Mission.
	Aug.	Elder A. Theodore Tuttle calls on Arturo Illia, president of Argentina.
1964		Monday night is designated for Family Home Evening. Richard G. Scott replaces Ronald V. Stone as president of the Argentina North Mission.
1965		First family home evening manuals published.
1966		Rex N. Terry is called as president of the Argentina Mission. Elders Richard L Evans and Franklin D. Richards visit the Argentina Mission.

xviii   History of the Mormons in Argentina

	May 1	The first stake in South America is organized in São Paulo, Brazil, with Walter Spät as president.
	Nov. 20	The Buenos Aires Stake is organized with Angel Abrea[1] as president.
1967	March	The Liahona is published in Spanish.
	Sept. 29	A new position of regional reprsentative of the Twelve was announced and the first sixty-nine regional representatives were called.
	Nov. 12	The Montevideo Stake is organized in Uruguay with Vicente Rubio as president.
1969		The first South America missionaries called to serve in Spain embark on their duties.
1970	Jan. 18	President David O. McKay dies and is succeeded by Joseph Fielding Smith, with Harold B. Lee, and N. Eldon Tanner as counselors.
1971		The Seminary program begins in Argentina, Uruguay, and Paraguay.
		-Church membership exceeds three million.
1972	Feb. 28	The Córdoba Argentina Stake is organized with Arturo Palmieri as president.
	March 1	The Mendoza Argentina Stake is organized with Mario A. Rastelli as president.
	July 2	President Joseph Fielding Smith dies and is succeeded by Harold B. Lee with N.

(1972)		Eldon Tanner and Marion G. Romney as counselors.
	July 30	The Argentina East Mission is split off from the Argentina North and South Missions. Joseph Bentley is its president.
1973	Dec. 26	President Harold B. Lee is succeeded by Spencer W. Kimball with the same counselors.
1974		President Kimball challenges members to "lengthen your stride," especially in regard to missionary work.
	May	The Buenos Aires West Stake is split off from the Buenos Aires Stake.
1975	March	An Area Conference is held in Buenos Aires for members of Argentina, Chile, Paraguay, and Uruguay. President Spencer W. Kimball announces the construction of the São Paulo Brazil Temple.
1976		The Missionary Training Center opens in Provo.
1978	June 1	President Spencer W. Kimball announces the revelation granting priesthood ordination to worthy men of all races.[2]
	Oct. 26-27	An Area General Conference in held in Montevideo.
	Oct. 28-29	An Area General Conference is held in Buenos Aires.

History of the Mormons in Argentina

	Oct 30	President Kimball dedicates the São Paulo Temple, Brazil.
	Dec. 15	Helvecio Martins is called to serve in the Rio de Janeiro Brazil Niteroi Stake presidency.[3]
1979		A new LDS edtion of the Kings James Version is published.
1981		A new edition of the triple combination is published.
		A satellite network is established to carry Church programs.
	April 4	Elder Angel Abrea of Argentina is called to the First Quorum of the Seventy.
1982	April 1	Worldwide Church membership exceeds five million.
1984	June 24	The First Presidency announces the organization of Area Presidencies.
	July	Members of the South American Area Presidency arrive in Buenos Aires: Elders A. Theodore Tuttle, Jacob de Jager, and Spencer H. Osborn.
	Aug.	Elders Boyd K. Packer and Bruce R. McConkie present the Buenos Aires Area Presidency.
1985	July	Elder J. Thomas Fyans is called as president of South America South Area.
	Aug. 16	Elder Angel Abrea arrives to preside over the Buenos Aires Temple.

	Nov. 5	President Spencer W. Kimball dies and is succeeded by Ezra Taft Benson with Gordon B. Hinckley and Thomas S. Monson as counselors.
	Dec.	The open house is held before the dedication of the Buenos Aires Temple.
1986	Jan.	President Thomas S. Monson dedicates the Lima Peru Temple and the Buenos Aires Temple.
	Jan. 20	The first proxy baptisms are held in the Buenos Aires Temple.
	Feb. 6	The Buenos Aires Missionary Training Center opens with Lyman Shreeve as president.
	Aug.	Elder Ted E. Brewerton is called as a counselor in the South America Area Presidency.
	Oct. 4	Stake quorum of the Seventy are discontinued.
1987	April	Elder Waldo P. Call is called as area president with counselors Elders John H. Groberg and L. Aldin Porter.
	July	Tomás F. Lindheimer and Carlos Agüero are called as mission presidents.[4]
	Aug.	Proxy baptisms for the dead reach one hundred million.
1989		The leaders of the Church in Buenos Aires meet separately with three Argentina presidential candidates: Eduardo Angeloz, Alvaro Alsogaray, and Carlos Menem.

xxii History of the Mormons in Argentina

	April	The Second Quorum of the Seventy is created.
1990	July	Missions are organized in Mendoza, Trelew, and Resistencia, Argentina.
	Oct. 1	Elder Jacob de Jager is called as area president with Elders Lynn A. Mickelsen and Eduardo Ayala[5] as counselors.
1991	Sept. 1	Church membership reaches eight million.
1992		Elder Lynn A. Mickelsen is called as area president with Elders Horacio A. Tenorio and John B. Dickson as counselors.
	Feb. 15	Groundbreaking ceremonies are held for the Buenos Aires Missionary Training Center and Temple Inn.
	Oct. 16	Uruguay's president, Dr. Luis Albert Lacalle, speaks at the Institute of Religion in Montevideo.
1993	Dec.	A new edition of the triple combination, including a topical index, is published in Spanish.
1994	May 30	President Ezra Taft Benson dies and is succeeded by Howard W. Hunter, with Gordon B. Hinckley and Thomas S. Monson as counselors.
1994	Dec. 11	The Church's two thousandth stake is created in Mexico.

1995	Jan.	Church membership reaches nine million members.
	March 3	President Howard W. Hunter dies and is succeeded by Gordon B. Hinckley with Thomas S. Monson and James E. Faust as counselors.
	April	Area Authorities replaces the calling of Regional Representatives.
	Dec.	Daniel Rodriguez de Almeida is named director of temporal affairs for the South America South Area.
1996	April 6	Francisco Viñes is called to the Second Quorum of the Seventy.
	Aug. 15	Elder John B. Dickson is called as area president, with Elders Carlos H. Amado and Hugo A. Catrón as counselors.
	Nov. 12	President Gordon B. Hinckley meets with fifty thousand Saints in Buenos Aires.
1997	April	The Third, Fourth, and Fifth Quorums of the Seventy are organized.
	Sept.	Elder Carlos H. Amado is called as president of the South America South Area with Elders Richard D. Allred and Hugo A. Catrón as counselors.

Notes

1. Angel Abrea grew up as a Church member when Latter-day Saints were a rarity in his country. There were perhaps four hundred members of the Church in Argentina when he was baptized at age ten, in November of 1943.

xxiv History of the Mormons in Argentina

But years of Church experience, combined with parental support, molded Angel Abrea into the kind of individual who could be a counselor in the district presidency at seventeen, and a branch president at twenty-three. He was later a district president, first stake president in his country, regional representative, and mission president before he was sustained as a member of the First Quorum of the Seventy on 4 April 1981. Searle, "Elder Angel Abrea," 25.

2. A little more than a year later, in June 1978, we received a telephone call from a friend in Salt Lake City, Utah, telling us that President Kimball had announced the revelation that all worthy males could hold the priesthood. I shall not forget that day. My wife cried. I cried. We knelt to thank our Heavenly Father. After that, the phone rang many, many times. Friends from the United States and Brazil called us. Janet Peterson and Helvecio Martins, "Friend to Friend," *Friend* (January 1992): 6.

3. During the cornerstone laying of the São Paulo Temple, President Spencer W. Kimball motioned for me to come to him. I looked around to see whom he was looking at. He repeated the gesture. I did not understand. James E. Faust looked at me and mouthed "come here. He wants to talk to you." I went. President Kimball shook my hand and took hold of my arm and said, "Brother, what is necessary for you is faithfulness. Remain faithful, and you will enjoy all the blessings of the Church." Peterson and Martins, "Friend to Friend," 6.

4. This emphasis on education and missions is paying off in Buenos Aires. "In the past it was not common to see young men serve missions," says Area Authority Seventy Carlos E. Agüero. "We are seeing change with the generations. Now young men and women are going by the hundreds. Education and mission goals are becoming the new tradition for Latter-day Saint youth." Olsen, "Argentina's Bright and Joyous Day," 32.

5. I grew up in Coronel, Chile. When I was seven years old, I memorized a poem of fourteen verses and recited it before an audience of twelve hundred people. After that experience I developed an increased desire to read more. I read about four little books a week. At that time my mother gave me a Bible. When I was twelve I read the Bible in about ten months. I was impressed with the history of the Old Testament and with the Atonement of the Savior in the New Testament. All my life I tried to find another book of scripture that would teach me more about these things. Janet Peterson and Eduardo Ayala, "Friend to Friend," *Friend* (March 1996): 6.

ILLUSTRATIONS

Parley P. Pratt	2
Dissidents' Cemetery, Valparaíso, Chile	4
Dissidents' Cemetery register	4
Sexton's registry at the Dissidents' Cemetery	6
Bay of Valparaíso	6
Parley P. Pratt	8
Rey L. Pratt	16
Trozos Selectos del Libro de Mormón, 1875	19
Melitón G. Trejo	20
Libro de Mormon, 1886	23
Revelacion de los Ultimos Dias	26
Doctrinas y Covenios, 1948	27
Melvin J. Ballard	32
Rulon S. Wells and Melvin J. Ballard	33
First group of Saints in South America	34
María M. Biébersdorf-Párraga and Edith Elisabeth Biébersdorf-Lencia	35
Missionaries in Parque Tres de Febrero	37
Missionary group	37
Reinhold Stoof and family	40
Evangelio Restaurado	41
Gianfelice family	43
Brothers Cuicci and Gianfelice	44
Antonino Gianfelice	44
Reinhold Stoof	46
Members meet Luacine and J. Reuben Clark, Ella and Reinhold Stoof	47
German members of White Branch	49
Lanús Sunday school	49
Eric Karl Fischer	50
Buenos Aires missionaries	61

xxvi   History of the Mormons in Argentina

Gerald O. Lynn	61
Elder Ostendorf and members	61
Branches and meeting houses in the Argentina Mission (1938)	62
Elder Ostendorf	62
Williams family	64
Scholz family house	64
Frederick S. Williams	66
Frederick S. Williams at Buenos Aires Temple dedication	66
Liniers Chapel under construction	69
Liniers Chapel	69
Samuel Boren and Lyman Shreeve	71
Antonino Gianfelice and R. G. Brewer	71
Roberto Pedro Antonietti	73
Antonino Gianfelice and R. G. Brewer	75
Luis Constantini and wife	75
James L. Barker	76
W. Ernest Young family	79
Fermín C. Barjollo	79
Samuel Boren	79
German members of White Branch	81
Missionaries in front of Quilmes Branch	81
Armin, María, and Dorotea Hofmann	82
Elisa Leonor Melga and Ramón Avila	88
Avila family	88
Ramón Avila	90
José Luis and Ana María Avila	92
Dömrose family	93
Dömrose couple	94
Parque San Martin Sunday School meeting	95
Robert E. Wells	98
El Mensajero Deseret	100
Thomas M. Looney and wife María A. Dido	105
Inés Looney Montani	106
Zaldivar family and Roberto Pedro Antonietti	108
Miguel Angel and Juan Carlos Avila	113
El Mensajero Deseret	116
David O. McKay with members	119
David O. McKay at Teatro Nacional Cervantes	119
David O. McKay speaking	120
President Ronald V. Stone and family	124

Illustrations   xxvii

North Argentina Mission leaders and wives	124
Statistics for December 31, 1962	125
Special Conference in Belgrano	127
Maipu, Córdoba Chapel	127
First missionaries in Salta	128
Gordon B. Hinckley at Tucumán chapel dedication	130
James Wilson with companion	132
Statistics and Missions	134
First baptismal service in Santiago	138
Harold B. Lee at mission home	139
Robert E. Wells	140
Richard G. Scott	140
Hugo N. Salvioli	141
Samuel Boren	141
Directive Council of Argentina Mission	144
Buenos Aires Stake Presidency	146
Caseros Chapel	146
Howard W. Hunter and H. Clay Gorton	148
Angel Fernández	148
Argentina South Mission Presidency	159
Henry D. Moyle	163
Ezra Taft Benson	163
Spencer W. Kimball	170
São Paulo Brazil Temple	173
Buenos Aires Temple groundbreaking ceremony	177
Buenos Aires Temple under construction	177
Bruce R. McConkie offering dedicatory prayer for Buenos Aires Temple	179
Groundbreaking ceremony, Buenos Aires Temple	179
Buenos Aires Temple Presidency	181
General Authorities at Buenos Aires Temple dedication	183
Buenos Aires Temple	185
A. Theodore Tuttle	192
J. Thomas Fyans	192
Waldo P. Call	192
Jacob de Jager	192
Lynn A. Mickelsen	193
John B. Dickson	193
Carlos H. Amado	193
Area Presidency (1986)	195
Area Presidency (1994)	195

xxviii   History of the Mormons in Argentina

Area Presidency (1997) 196
Gabriel Saez 203
Area Presidency with Area Seventy Authorities 203
Missionaries in Ushuaia 211
Choir in Vélez Sarsfield Stadium 213
Gordon B. Hinckley with stake presidents of Buenos Aires 213
Gordon B. Hinckley 215

INTRODUCTION

Well-known since its origin in 1830 as the Mormon Church, The Church of Jesus Christ of Latter-day Saints was established in Argentina in 1925.

Since the first missionaries arrived in Buenos Aires to initiate the preaching of the gospel, the Church has steadily maintained a significant presence in the country—within decades, extending over several nations of Latin America. With slow initial growth, the missionaries built the base that presently sustains more than two million Saints in South America. In 1925 there were approximately five hundred thousand worldwide members of the Church. Today [2003], after eighty years, there are more than eleven million members worldwide with over three hundred thousand of those members residing in Argentina.

The first missionaries from the Church to arrive in Argentina proclaimed their beliefs with respect to the existing religions, ministers, and members. The eleventh Article of Faith written by the Prophet Joseph Smith in 1843 was consistently exercised:

> We claim the privilege of worshiping Almighty God according to the dictates of our own conscience, and allow all men the same privilege, let them worship how, where, or what they may.

Mormonism makes an open and welcome acknowledgement to the groups and religious persons who, throughout the centuries, have promoted faith in Christ and Christian values while also expressing admiration and support for faith and righteousness as opposed to the advancement of sin and evil in the modern-day world.

With relation to the government and its policies, the Church maintains an impartial position as far as the various political parties, encouraging its members to fulfill all their civil obligations as described in the twelfth Article of Faith. "We believe in being subject to kings, presidents, rulers, and magistrates, in obeying, honoring, and sustaining the law."

A HISTORY OF FAITH

This book is the story of the establishment and expansion of The Church of Jesus Christ of Latter-day Saints in Argentina. It focuses primarily on the faith and experiences of individuals and how religion motivated and changed their lives. Included are stories and histories of families and persons who have been instrumental in the establishment of the Church in Argentina.

BEFORE ARRIVING IN ARGENTINA

The beginning of the restoration of The Church of Jesus Christ of Latter-day Saints on the earth commenced with Joseph Smith's First Vision, traditionally dated as the spring of 1820. The Father and the Son appeared to the young Prophet Joseph in a wooded area near Manchester, New York. In 1829 Joseph continued the translation and publication of the Book of Mormon and the restoration of the priesthood.

With April 6, 1830, being the official organizational date for The Church of Jesus Christ of Latter-day Saints, the twenty years that followed were perhaps the most challenging in

Introduction xxxi

Mormon history. In 1831, persecution followed the Saints from New York to Kirtland, Ohio, and then on to Independence, Missouri. Soon expelled to the northern part of the state of Missouri, they traveled to Nauvoo, Illinois in 1838–39.

In 1844 the Prophet Joseph Smith and his brother Hyrum were assassinated in the jail at Carthage, Illinois. Two years later, following turmoil over the management of the Church, Brigham Young emerged as the clear leader over the largest group of Saints. As a result of continued persecution, the Saints were expelled again. This time it was toward the west, to the Rocky Mountains, with the first company of pioneers arriving in the Salt Lake valley in July 1847, and founding Salt Lake City.

Since that time, the world headquarters of The Church of Jesus Christ of Latter-day Saints has remained in Utah, with great missionary efforts being directed toward all nations of the world.

The preaching of the gospel remained the central foundational base in the early Church. Throughout the first decade after the restoration of the Church, missionaries were dispatched to other continents. The activity of the missionaries in Europe resulted in a large number of converts immigrating and uniting with the body of the Church in Salt Lake City.

With the arrival of the twentieth century, important changes were made. Missionaries no longer encouraged converts to gather to Salt Lake City, but to remain in their native countries in order to help build the Church and spread the gospel.[1] The Church continued to grow in numbers and in experience, preparing the members to share the gospel of Jesus Christ with everyone on the earth. As the Church further increased in size and resources, missionaries were called from the United States and other strongholds of the Church to serve in faraway lands.

In 1925 it was the decision of the First Presidency of the Church to open the South America Mission. For this purpose three missionaries were sent to the city of Buenos Aires,

Argentina. Those missionaries were Melvin J. Ballard of the Quorum of the Twelve Apostles, and Rulon S. Wells and Rey L. Pratt of the First Council of the Seventy. Several important events which occurred that contributed to the arrival of the Church in South America were: Parley P. Pratt's mission to Chile in 1851, establishment of the Church in Mexico in 1876, Thomas S. Page and Andrew Jenson's[2] exploratory trip to South America, and the establishment of freedom of religious worship in different countries.

The history of the Church in Argentina is intertwined with the history of both South America and Latin America. Their antecedent details are closely tied to each other, due to common culture, language, and history.

Notes

    1. "Unbeknown to themselves the nations of the world were under divine direction to assist this expansion, while Church authorities felt that 'as occasion justifies the action, undoubtedly temples will be built in various parts of the earth, for the further salvation of the children of men.'" Douglas James Davies, *Mormon Spirituality: Latter Day Saints in Wales and Zion* (Nottingham U.K.: University of Nottingham, 1987), 112.

    2. In 1925, seventy-five years after Pratt's mission to Chile, a second effort was attempted when the First Presidency assigned Andrew Jenson and Thomas S. Page to tour South America to review the possibility of opening it to missionary work. Their report was favorable and the Council of the Twelve gave unanimous approval to organize a mission. http://www.asquared.com/inetpub/URUMission/history/index.asp.

Chapter 1

THE PACIFIC MISSION

Immediately after the arrival and settlement of the Saints in the Salt Lake valley in 1847, the Church renewed its efforts of preaching the gospel by sending missionaries to some of the remotest points on earth.

Parley P. Pratt, a very prominent leader and member of the Quorum of the Twelve Apostles, was sent to direct the work in the Pacific Islands, the lower portion of California, and South America. Pratt, who was baptized a member of the Church in September 1830, was a close friend of Joseph Smith. As a high-ranking leader in the Restoration, Pratt participated in many major events during the three decades that spanned from the organization of the Church in New York, to the definitive establishment of the headquarters in Salt Lake City.

When Pratt was appointed to the presidency of the Pacific Mission, the mission at that time encompassed all the islands and coasts of the Pacific. He recounted the direction he received from the First Presidency:

> I hold the presidency of all the islands and coasts of the Pacific, under the direction of the First Presidency of the Church—to open the door to every nation and tongue, as fast

2 History of the Mormons in Argentina

Parley P. Pratt

as the way is prepared and the Lord directs, for the preaching of the gospel of salvation.[1]

The Trip to Chile

After directing the departure of missionaries to the Pacific Islands, Elder Pratt started for South America. On September 5, 1851, the ship *Henry Kelsey*[2] embarked from San Francisco on a journey to Valparaíso, Chile. Aboard were Pratt, accompanied by his wife Phoebe Sopher, who was in an advanced state of pregnancy, and fellow missionary Rufus Allen. Several in the group fell ill due to shortages of food on the lengthy marine voyage. Sixty-four days after embarking, the group disembarked in Valparaíso on November 8, with no one in the party being able to speak the local language. In a letter written to his family in Utah, Elder Pratt attempted to express his frustration with these words:

> Well, dear ones, six months have passed, and their events have been recorded in the records of eternity since we parted; all this time I have had not one lisp from you. Oh, how lonesome! Just imagine the monotony! Sky and sea! Sea and sky! Night and day! Day and night! Infinitude of space! Boundless waste! Emblem of eternal silence! Eternal banishment! Eternal loneliness, where the voice of the bridegroom and of the bride are not heard. Where the holy music of children's voices, in joyous merriment, falls not on the ear….
>
> We have a miser for a captain, who thinks more of a six-pence than he does of our lives or even of his own. He will not suffer the steward to cook potatoes, bread, pies, puddings or any other wholesome food, but keeps us on hard, mouldy bread, full of bugs and worms, and on salt beef and pork—the pork being rotten.[3]

4   History of the Mormons in Argentina

Dissidents' Cemetery, Valparaíso, Chile.

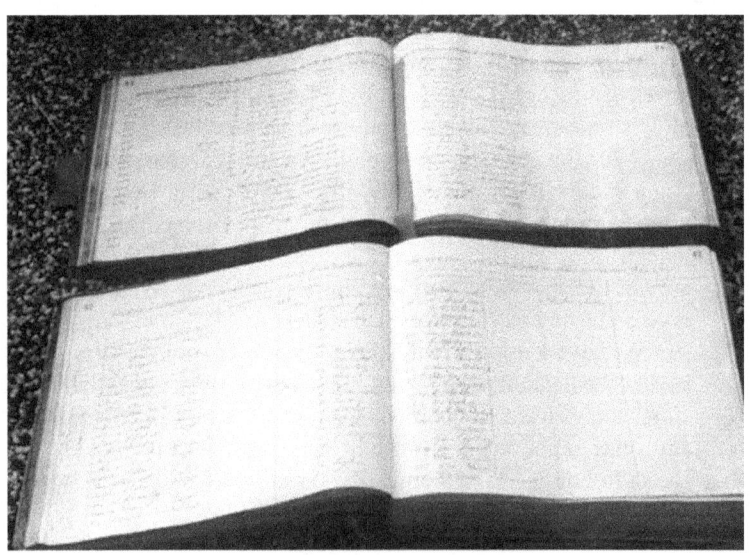

Dissidents' Cemetery register.

On arrival they lodged at a French hotel located a few blocks from the wharf. Soon after, they bought furniture and rented a house in a local neighborhood on Victoria Street. They dedicated themselves to the study of the Spanish language while learning the customs, culture, and history of the country.

At that time, Elder Pratt's visit to Chile did not lead to the permanent establishment of the Church in South America. Pratt did not hold public meetings nor did he make any official contact with the government to initiate the work. Therefore, there were no converts. Nevertheless, following the trail of this great missionary on his trip to South America increases our esteem of Pratt and allows us to appreciate the value of his life and character. Despite adversity, he stands as an example of dedication to the work and as a great leader with an unshakable testimony.

While preparing to return to the United States, in a letter dated March 13, 1852, to Brigham Young, Elder Pratt relayed the following:

> The civil wars, and my own pecuniary circumstances, but more particularly the want of language, prevented my travelling much in the country, or even visiting the Arraucanians. I, however, visited a small town in the interior, forty miles, and lived there one month.
>
> On the second day of March we embarked on this ship bound for San Francisco, without a sufficiency of the language to turn the keys of the Gospel as yet to these nations. We staid till all our means were exhausted and sought and prayed diligently for our way to open; but we could neither speak the language sufficiently to preach the Gospel nor find any way to earn our living, so we found it necessary to return to California while we still study the language on board.[4]

The Death of Omner Pratt

On November 30, 1851, three weeks after arriving in Valparaíso, Phoebe S. Pratt gave birth to a son, Omner. Five

6   History of the Mormons in Argentina

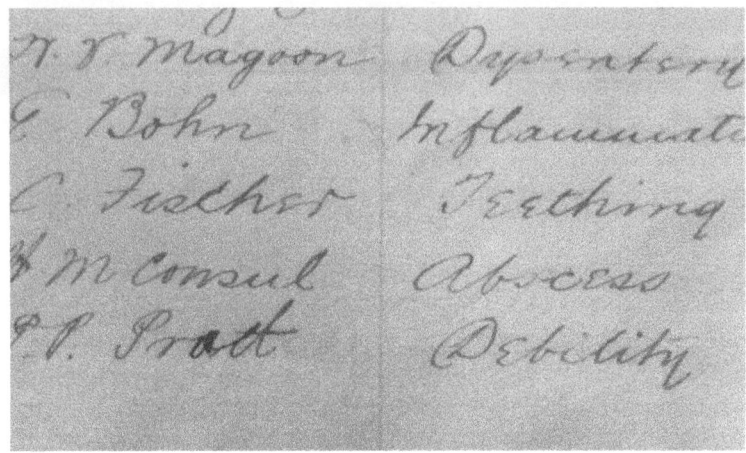

The name Parley P. Pratt appears in the sexton's registry with the cause of his son Omner's death, "Debility." This register is located in the Dissidents Cemetery office at Valparaíso.

The Bay of Valparaíso today. This is where Parley P. Pratt arrived in 1851.

weeks later on January 7, 1852, the small boy passed away due to an illness.[5] Omner was buried at the top of the hills in Valparaíso.

In addition to the tragic loss of Omner Pratt, there was the added challenge of beginning the work of spreading the gospel in Chile. A few days after the child's death, the missionaries moved to the city of Quillota, forty-four miles from Valparaíso. This move, probably in search of a more propitious place, would provide a more stable atmosphere than the one offered by the harbor city:

> We departed from Valparaíso in a cart drawn by oxen, and arrived on the morning of the twenty-fifth at Quillota—a small town situated in a beautiful and fertile valley on a river thirty-six miles from Valparaíso.[6]

A Month in Quillota

They remained in the city of Quillota for a month, studying Spanish and looking for opportunities to preach the gospel. In the autobiography of Parley P. Pratt, the following excerpt is found:

> The people in this town seem to be a neat, plain, loving and sociable people; very friendly, frank, and easy to become acquainted with.
> A mountain or round hill perhaps 500 feet high, rises in the midst of the town, and is surrounded on all sides by the level of the fertile, well watered and well cultivated plain. This hill is near our residence, easy of access, and commands a view of the whole valley with its farms, orchards, vineyards, towns, streets, river and water ditches, fertile as Eden and stretching away till lost in the dim distance; or bounded by lofty hills and mountain chains, whose lower swells are checked with fences and houses, and covered with flocks and herds....

8   History of the Mormons in Argentina

Parley P. Pratt praying on Mayaca Hill, Quillota, as interpreted by the Argentinean painter Jorge Cocco.

The whole taken in at one view from the summit of the center hill, presents one of the most beautiful scenes I ever beheld in the old or new world.

On the top of this mountain is a place for retirement and prayer, which I intend to use every evening about sunset or dusk. Figs, plums, pears, peaches, apples, oranges, grapes, and, indeed, most kinds of fruit are very plentiful here.[7]

The Return to California

After a brief time in Valparaíso and Quillota, Elders Pratt and Allen made the decision to return to the United States. It had not been possible to preach the gospel or establish a branch of the Church. The voyage home was expected to be as difficult as the voyage to Chile. Elder Pratt described the group's rough travel across the Pacific Ocean toward California on the ship *Dracut*:[8]

> Fifty-five days have passed like a dreary imprisonment to us, with but little to eat. We live on a little poor, hard bread, probably baked some two or three years ago, and some beans, and very poor damaged salt beef and pork. We have had no flour, potatoes, sugar, molasses, rice, or other comforts, although we pay a good price for cabin passage.
>
> We have not had one day of good sailing in month; it is either calms or light head winds. We seldom sail more than from thirty to fifty miles in twenty-four hours. We are hungry, weary, lonesome, and disconsolate. But, after praying much for a fair wind and speed, we find our prayers are not answered, and we have given it up, and have asked our Heavenly Father to give us patience and reconciliation to His will.
>
> We are now some eight or nine hundred miles from port and our provisions (poor as they are) must fail us soon. But live or die we trust in God and try to serve Him.
>
> Brethren, I want to see you all with a desire above all other times of my life. I feel as though I wanted to sit down with you and seek the powers and gifts of God and the powers of Heaven, even that which shall be shed forth for the restoration of the house of Israel.[9]

An Apostle's Vision

In the same letter to Brigham Young, Elder Pratt expressed the following:

> I hope I shall not be counted a slothful servant; for I assure you that I do all in my power, with all diligence, and with all the prayer of faith I possess; and my earnest desire is to be counted worthy to labor for the restoration of Israel until it be accomplished.

10   History of the Mormons in Argentina

> I study the language all day and think of it, and even dream and talk it aloud in my sleep, in which I sometimes learn more than in the day.
>
> I feel that the Book of Mormon and some cheap publications should be translated into Spanish and printed, and then the key be turned to these nations while a living Priesthood is accompanied by something for them to read—even those writings which have the promises of God, the prayers and faith of the ancients, and the power and Spirit of God to work with them in restoring the house of Israel.
>
> As these contemplated labors would be under the blessing of God, a furtherance of the great work of laying the foundation for the restoration of unnumbered millions of the house of Israel and of Joseph—even of many nations extending over a large and important portion of the earth—I feel to labor with patience, and to take time to prepare the way before me and before those who will, in due time, be sent unto them in power; knowing that God, who has said certain things, will cause those things to be performed in due time.[10]

The Situation in Chile in 1851

In his book, *Los Mormones in Chile*, Rodolfo Acevedo describes what the time period was like in the history of the country:

> In the first decades of the nineteenth century, a brief time preceding independence, the first protestant outposts were established in the country. These outposts were built primarily through the work of the *colportores*, or traveling Bible salesmen, who were dedicated to distributing and spreading the book among the population.
>
> With the establishment of English churches in Chile, the first ministers arrived in 1837. Their primary aim was caring for the spiritual needs of those associated with the Anglican faith who resided in Valparaíso.

The Pacific Mission   11

Another Protestant faith established in the country in the middle of the nineteenth century was Lutheran, which arrived with the first group of immigrants from Germany, settling in the south part of Chile. Previously, few individual German families who professed the Lutheran faith were in the country.

Even though the Anglican and the Lutheran were not proselytizing churches, they were still troubling to the Catholic hierarchy of those days. The Catholic Church was and is the predominant faith of the nation. The constitution of 1833 in its third chapter and fifth article declares that, "the religion of the Republic of Chile is the catholic, apostolic, Roman Church; and excludes the public exercise of any other."

David Trumbull,[11] an outstanding individual among the Protestant leaders in the middle of the nineteenth century, pleaded intensely for freedom of religion and the representation of various denominations in Chile. He arrived in the country in 1845 and founded the Union Church, a North American congregational church. He tended to attract members of the different Protestant denominations, essentially from the United States, that had little representation in the country. The faithful of the Union Church were, in his opinion, the sailors or crew on many of the foreign boats that arrived in Valparaíso. This meant that the congregation of the Union Church was constantly renewing the faithful members after the docking or arrival of a boat. In fact, David Trumbull initiated his proselytizing work in Chile while preaching to sailors on board a boat.

Later Trumbull published the newspaper *El Mercurio* of Valparaíso. Translated as *The Neighbor*, it was published in English and appealed for freedom of religion and the representation of various denominations. That religious freedom would not be obtained until 1865 with the revision and new interpretation of the fifth article of the constitution.[12]

12   History of the Mormons in Argentina

Notes

1. Parley P. Pratt, Jr, ed., *Autobiography of Parley P. Pratt* (Salt Lake City: Deseret Book, 1994), 384.

2. On September 5, 1851, the *Henry Kelsey* left San Francisco under the command of Captain C. E. Sampson, taking sixty-four days to reach Valparaíso, Chile. It was a barkentine vessel which was the typical cargo-carrier of the early twentieth century. http://www.maritimeheritage.org.

3. Pratt, *Autobiography,* 388, 390.

4. Ibid., 397.

5. The sexton's registry at the Dissidents' Cemetery in Valparaíso lists "debility" as the cause of Omner's death.

6. Pratt, *Autobiography,* 394.

7. Ibid., 395.

8. On May 20, 1852, the *Dracut* left Valparaíso, Chile, under the command of Captain Loper, taking seventy-five days to reach its destination. It was a brigantine vessel, carrying a cargo of coal and ten passengers: Mr. P. Pratt and lady, R. Allen, J. Brown, M. Lopez, J. Beal, A. Ryard, P. Rello, R. Lord, and J. Loomis. http://www.maritimeheritage.org.

9. Pratt, *Autobiography,* 403.

10. Ibid., 401.

11. Chilean Presbyterianism began with the arrival of David Trumbull to Chile in 1845. He was sent by the American and Foreign Missions Society of the Congregational Churches in the United States. He began his work in Valparaíso, Chile, and was the first Protestant in Chile to engage in evangelism of the Spanish-speaking population. http://www.reformiert-online.net.

12. Rodolfo Acevedo, *Los Mormones en Chile: 30 años de la Iglesia de Jesucristo de los Santos de los Últimos Días, 1956–1986.* (Santiago: Imprenta Cumora, 1990), 10–11.

Chapter 2

BEGINNING THE WORK IN MEXICO

During the October 1875 general conference held in Salt Lake City, several men were called to aid in opening the Mexico Mission. Those serving as missionaries were: Daniel W. Jones,[1] James Z. Stewart, Helaman Pratt,[2] Wiley C. Jones, Robert H. Smith, Ammon M. Tenney,[3] and Anthony W. Ivins.

On September 1, 1875, those who had received the call to serve in Mexico were given further instructions to meet in the small town of Nephi, Utah, in order to make preparations to travel to Mexico. The missionaries who undertook the march on their exploratory mission were to go to the Mexican prairies where the Lamanites lived. In addition, they were given instructions to travel only by land, to explore the regions south of the state of Utah, and to enter by the state of Sonora. Jacob Hamblin accompanied them as a guide and an interpreter until they crossed the Colorado River.[4]

A partial list of the items that they took consisted of two thousand *Trozos Selectos del Libro de Mormón*, twenty mules, equipment to encamp, and supplies to properly maintain the animals on the journey. Additionally, an assortment of dehydrated food, including fruits, was packed for the trip.

It was January 7, 1876, when the first missionaries in the dispensation of the fullness of times entered Mexico. It is interesting to note that when they crossed the border, these men of God looked over their shoulders with a minimal amount of concern and fear. They worried that the adversary would do something to prevent what they felt was the miracle of the Book of Mormon from finally entering into Mexico.[5]

After several frustrating experiences dealing with local officials, they received permission in Chihuahua to hold a public meeting, and on April 8, 1876, they preached to a group of approximately five hundred persons at the first LDS meeting in the interior of Mexico. After some other attempts to preach the gospel, they returned to the United States, arriving in Salt Lake City on July 5, 1876.[6]

A second mission to Mexico was served in 1876–77. It was composed of two of the original missionaries, Stewart and Pratt, and four new ones, Stewart's brother Isaac, George Terry, Louis Garff, and Melitón G. Trejo.

The development of the Church in Mexico was facilitated by three main factors which also contributed to the establishment of the Church in South America:

First came the initial translation and printing of Church materials into Spanish. It was necessary to obtain resources such as pamphlets and tracts containing a basic knowledge of the culture and circumstances in which the missionaries could communicate the message in order to develop Christ's work.

Second, the Book of Mormon was translated into Spanish. Obviously, the preaching of the restored gospel without the Book of Mormon was very difficult, something which Parley P. Pratt had clearly understood. When leaving Chile, he penned the following to Brigham Young:

> I feel that the Book of Mormon and other less expensive publications must be translated and printed in the Spanish lan-

guage in order to turn the key for the preaching of the gospel in these nations.

Third was the influence of the Saints from the colonies of northern Mexico. Due to the prohibition of plural marriage resulting from recently passed laws in the United States, families exiled from Utah became the ones establishing these colonies.

The laws that were instituted against the practice of plural marriage in the United States increased the antagonism and prejudice directed toward the Church. The federal government seized Church-owned goods and properties in Utah, eliminated the female vote, and "...embarked on a campaign of unrelenting persecution directed against all the members of the Church that had entered into marriages with plural spouses."

"It is almost unbelievable that these atrocities took place in the United States in 1887 as opposed to Spain or Holland in the days of the Inquisition."[7]

In 1885 hundreds of families who practiced plural marriage crossed the border into Mexico. During the following years they founded the colonies of Díaz, Dublan, Juárez, Pacheco, García, Chuichupa, Oaxaca, and Morelos.

The Mormon colonies of Mexico prospered and the populations increased.[8] Growth evolved out of the trials they had weathered while colonizing the arid Salt Lake valley in Utah. As a result of that experience they brought to Mexico a great variety of fruit trees along with a channel irrigation system. They constructed schools and homes. Like Utah, the northern part of Mexico began to bloom like a desert rose.

By the end of the century the population of the colonies had grown to over five thousand. Six of the twelve Apostles had recently resided there or were currently living in one of the colonies. On December 8, 1895, the first stake was organized in Juárez, Mexico, with Anthony W. Ivins as president.[9]

16   History of the Mormons in Argentina

Beginning in 1925, authorities sent Rey L. Pratt to Argentina. In 1935 W. Ernest Young was called as the first Argentina Mission president. Since that time, thousands of men of South American descent have traveled to Argentina, being called as missionaries, mission presidents, temple officials, and even General Authorities. Many South American Latter-day Saints continue to feel that the leadership, dedication, and effort of these individuals still leave a profound mark on the Saints of their country.

Rey L. Pratt

Looking at South America

Joseph Smith made a very interesting declaration when he stated that all of the territory of the Americas, including Central and South, was a part of Zion. Moreover, there is sufficient evidence to support that the early leaders of the Church also considered South America an extremely important land.

In August 1841, in Brigham Young's home in Nauvoo, B. H. Roberts made reference to a meeting of the Quorum of the Twelve, where it was approved that "Elder Harrison Sagers proceed immediately on his mission to Jamaica, West Indies, and Elder Joseph Ball to South America."[10]

No other references exist as to the mission of Elder Ball in South America. Possibly his destination was changed but there is no indication of the ultimate outcome of his mission.

Unfortunately, the time for the restored gospel to be introduced in South America had not yet arrived. Perhaps it was because the existing conditions that were faced were not in their favor. When the first missionaries of the Church left Missouri and Illinois toward different parts of the world, the South American nations were in the middle of an attempt to gain their independence from Spain and other European powers.

When Parley P. Pratt was sent to the Pacific and South America in 1851 he was given instructions to "open the door to every nation and tongue as fast as the way is prepared." Unfortunately, it was not possible to begin the work in a consistent and definitive form.

It took more than seventy years for the Church to stabilize and for the political environment to reach a point where one could say "the way was prepared."

The Translation of the Book of Mormon into Spanish

Nephi states in the Book of Mormon:

> And it came to pass that I, Nephi, said unto my father: I will go and do the things which the Lord hath commanded, for I know that the Lord giveth no commandments unto the children of men, save he shall prepare a way for them that they may accomplish the thing which he commandeth them. [1 Ne. 3:7]

The history of the first translation of the Book of Mormon into Spanish is an example of how the way was prepared for the spreading of the Church in South America.

Today, the translation of the Book of Mormon into a new language is not a significant challenge or insurmountable task. The Church has developed an extensive translation department which clearly was not available in years past. There exists a story of faith and sacrifice behind the translation of the Book of Mormon into Spanish. It was in 1886 that Melitón G. Trejo and James Z. Stewart completed the translation.

The Conversion of Melitón González Trejo

Melitón González Trejo was born on March 10, 1843, in Garganta-La-Olla, Cáceres, in the western part of Spain. He was a descendant of the Trejo family whose ancestors arrived in Spain during the time of the Roman Empire. Many of their family were great military leaders who were involved in the religious history of Spain. Among them, Don Pedro Fernando de Trejo, a general of the armies of the kingdom of Galicia and assistant captain of King Fernando in the Battle of Seville, achieved a victory that contributed to the foundation of the new state of Spain. After the conquest, Don Pedro Fernando de Trejo established his residence

Trozos Selectos del Libro de Mormón, 1875

Melitón G. Trejo

in the valley of Concha, near the city of Burgos, in Castilla la Vieja. Later, the family moved to the west of Spain. While serving as bishop, Antonio de Trejo left Cartagena in 1618 because he was appointed Franciscan Commissioner to the Indians. Counted among their relatives was a cardinal of the Catholic Church and many others who participated in the military and religious conquest of the New World.

With this illustrious ancestry, Melitón G. Trejo was able to enjoy many advantages. He pursued a military career, graduated from a military academy as a lieutenant with a liberal education, served as an official in the Tropas Reales, and later, received his doctorate from the University of Bordeaux in France. Melitón's high-quality education combined with the wealth and prominence of his father's family, afforded him much prestige.

Beginning the Work in Mexico 21

In spite of his active military life, Melitón searched continuously for religious direction. Still, he seemed to gain no satisfactory answers from people or books. While listening to a companion speak about a group of Saints in the Rocky Mountains that had been directed there by a Prophet of God, Melitón was suddenly filled with the desire to find this group of people. He requested permission from the queen to accompany an expedition that would leave on a course to the Philippines, hoping in the process to find an opportunity to visit America, specifically Salt Lake City.

Because of the heavy workload, Melitón seemed to have briefly forgotten the key reason for his trip to the Philippines until an unfortunate illness forced him to recuperate in bed. It was during his recovery that he was provided with the time to contemplate. Deciding to resume his primary objective and to undertake a trip to the Rocky Mountains, in fervent prayer he asked God to help him find the truth he was seeking and to make God's will known to him.

That night Melitón had a dream that he considered very sacred, one which he apparently never revealed to anyone, except possibly Brigham Young.

After making arrangements with the army, obtaining money, and fixing his passage, Melitón started for America. Disembarking in San Francisco on July 4, 1874, he then traveled on to Salt Lake City. Although he had received a first-class education, he never really had the opportunity to practice his knowledge of the English language. In his mind this language barrier would present great difficulty in finding and recognizing the truth that he had been searching for.

While walking down the streets of Salt Lake City dressed in his Spanish uniform, he caught the attention of Brother Blanchard. Brother Blanchard was a native of France and professor of romance languages at Brigham Young Academy.

Additionally, he was fluent in Spanish; therefore he could speak to Melitón in his native tongue. Without delay Melitón made his intentions known. Brother Blanchard taught him the restored gospel, then introduced him to Brigham Young and other Church leaders. Melitón felt he had finally found the one true gospel he had been searching for.

Melitón told his life story to President Young, which included his dream and his desire to translate the Book of Mormon into Spanish. This would then allow him to take the gospel back to his hometown.

Using his hard-earned money, Brother Trejo, along with Daniel W. Jones, worked on translating selections from the Book of Mormon into Spanish. They completed this work in 1875. It was published under the title of *Trozos Selectos del Libro de Mormón* (*Selections from the Book of Mormon*). After this first publication, Brother Trejo found himself translating *A Voice of Warning*, written by Parley P. Pratt. These works were presented to the Church as a gift of gratitude for the joy and happiness the gospel had brought to Melitón in his life. Melitón had started with two thousand dollars; now he had not more than fifty cents left in his pocket. However, this loss of financial security was gladly replaced by his overwhelming satisfaction at his accomplishment.

In October 1876, Brother Trejo was called to the Mexico Mission. Returning in 1877, he was called again in 1879 to a second mission to Mexico. In 1884 Elder Trejo married Emily Jones in the Logan Temple. Soon after, when the Latter-day Saints established their colonies in Mexico, Melitón was set apart as a missionary and would go on to serve in that capacity for the next nine years.

In 1883, under the supervision of Moses Thatcher[11] and the Quorum of the Twelve, along with the aid of James Z. Stewart, Elder Trejo completed the entire translation of the Book

LIBRO DE MORMON:

RELACION ESCRITA POR

LA MANO DE MORMON,

SOBRE

PLANCHAS TOMADAS DE LAS PLANCHAS
DE NEFI.

Por tanto es un compendio de los análes del pueblo de Nefi, y tambien de los Lamanitas, escrito para los Lamanitas, quienes son un resto de la casa de Israel; y tambien para los Jodíos y Gentiles: escrito por via de mandamiento y por el Espíritu de profecía y revelacion. Siendo escrito, sellado, y escondido para el Señor, para que no fuese destruido; para que apareciere por el don y poder de Dios para su interpretacion; sellado por la mano de Moroni y escondido para el Señor á fin de que reparecière á su debido tiempo por medio de los Gentiles. Cuya interpretacion se daiá por el don de Dios.

Y tambien un compendio del libro de Éther; el cual es la historia de los del Pueblo de Jared; quienes fueron dispersados en la época de la confusion de las lenguas del pueblo, cuando estaban construyendo una Torre para llegar al cielo: lo que es para mostrar al resto de la casa de Israel, cuan grandes cosas ha hecho el Señor para sus padres; y para que conozcan las alianzas del Señor, y vean que no han sido desechados para siempre; y tambien para convencer á los Judíos y Gentiles de que Jesus es el Cristo, el Dios Eterno, que se manifiesta á sí mismo á todas las naciones. Y ahora si hay faltas, son equivocaciones de los hombres; por lo tanto, no condenéis las cosas de Dios, para que aparezcáis sin mancha ante el tribunal de Cristo.

TRADUCIDO POR JOSEPH SMITH, JUNIOR.

TRADUCIDO AL ESPAÑOL BAJO LA DIRECCION DEL

APÓSTOL MOISÉS THATCHER,

POR

MELITON G. TREJO Y JÁIME Z. STEWART.

IMPRESO Y PUBLICADO POR LA COMPAÑÍA DE DESERET NEWS, EN LA
CIUDAD DE SALT LAKE, UTAH, ESTADOS UNIDOS DE AMÉRICA.

1886.

The first translation of the Book of Mormon in Spanish, printed in 1886

of Mormon. In 1886 the first copy was published in Salt Lake City. President Rey L. Pratt, one of the Seven Presidents of the First Council of the Seventy, later reviewed the edition in 1922, and again in 1929. In 1952 a new corrected and revised edition was authorized. Then in 1992 a completely new translation with chapter headings and footnotes similar to the current English edition was completed.

The conversion of Melitón G. Trejo is not often mentioned in the history of the Church. However, considering the circumstances surrounding these events, I consider him relevant and heroic. He was a young Spanish military man, who lived half the nineteenth century with his family roots and nationalistic traditions. He listened to stories of the Saints and the Prophet in the Rocky Mountains. He read pamphlets distributed by the Church, but had still not met a missionary or heard the preaching of the gospel. Accordingly, he had no acquaintance with any members in the Church before arriving in Salt Lake City. As a result of a few simple references, Melitón had an overwhelming desire to become acquainted and join with the Saints; so strong was the desire that Melitón sailed half the world, losing family, friends, and a privileged position in the army of Spanish Corona to realize his dream.

Great accomplishments of Melitón G. Trejo included the translation of the Book of Mormon into the Spanish language and his extraordinary pioneering missionary work for the Church in Mexico.

The descendants of Melitón settled in Arizona and various places where the Church was already established. The influence of this pioneer has since been multiplied greatly, resulting in the large numbers of his decendents witnessed today. Melitón G. Trejo can be considered a great Spanish influence, a pioneer of the Church, and a hero of the Restoration in the latter days.

The Translation of the Doctrine and Covenants and the Pearl of Great Price

For many years the only writings that Spanish-speaking Latin America had access to had been the Bible and the Book of Mormon. However, 1930 was marked by the fulfillment of the promise in Doctrine and Covenants 90:11:

> For it shall come to pass in that day, that every man shall hear the fulness of the gospel in his own tongue, and in his own language.

In 1887, selections from the Doctrine and Covenants had been translated and published in Mexico by Horacio Cummings and Fernando A. Lara.

Rey L. Pratt, who served as president of the Mexico Mission, began the translation of *Latter-day Revelations* into Spanish. Elder Pratt had lived in Mexico as a young man and, in 1906, was called there to be a missionary. In 1907 he was called to preside over the Mexico Mission and, in 1925, was called to the First Council of the Seventy.

The end of 1930 saw the completion of President Pratt's translation of *Latter-day Revelations* into Spanish. It was being reviewed and prepared for publication at the time of his death in April 1931. Coincidently, the next mission president, Antoine R. Ivins, was also proficient in the Spanish language. He continued revising the work started by President Pratt and after completion, the book entitled *Revelaciones del los Ultimos Dias* was published in 1933 in Los Angeles.

In January 1934, President Antoine R. Ivins returned to Salt Lake City to assume his responsibility in the First Quorum of the Seventy. Feeling that the time had arrived for Spanish-speaking Saints to have a complete volume of the revelations, he obtained permission to continue the work and began to translate the portions that had not been included in the first edition.

REVELACION DE LOS ULTIMOS DIAS

Selecciones del
LIBRO DE DOCTRINAS Y CONVENIOS
de
LA IGLESIA DE JESUCRISTO DE LOS SANTOS DE LOS ÚLTIMOS DÍAS

Contiene revelaciones dadas por medio de
JOSÉ SMITH, EL PROFETA.

Traducido por   Rey L. Pratt
                  Antoine R. Ivins

Publicadas por

La Misión Mexicana de la Iglesia de Jesucristo de los Santos de los Últimos Días.

Los Angeles, California, E. U. A.
1933.

Selections from the Doctrine and Covenants, translated into Spanish beginning in 1930, and printed in 1933.

LAS
DOCTRINAS Y CONVENIOS

DE

LA IGLESIA DE JESUCRISTO
DE LOS SANTOS DE LOS ULTIMOS DIAS

Contiene Revelaciones Dadas a
JOSE SMITH, EL PROFETA

Con Algunos Aditamentos de sus Sucesores
en la Presidencia de la Iglesia

PUBLICACION DE
La Iglesia de Jesucristo de los Santos de los Ultimos Dias
SALT LAKE CITY, UTAH, E.U.A.
1948

First Spanish edition of the Docritne and Covenants, published in 1948

In 1948, with careful comparisons and revisions by aid of Eduardo Balderas, the Spanish edition of the Doctrine and Covenants was published in its entirety. While the type was being set for the Doctrine and Covenants, thought was given as to the translation of the Pearl of Great Price.[12] It was decided that it would be included in the same volume as the Doctrine and Covenants.

With the publication of the Doctrine and Covenants and the Pearl of Great Price in 1948, all four of the standard works were now available to Spanish-speaking people throughout the world, affording them the opportunity to hear these scriptures "in [their] own tongue, and in their own language."[13]

Notes

1. Orphaned at the age of eleven, Daniel Webster Jones launched himself west in 1847 with a company of Missouri Volunteers, off to fight in the Mexican War. Jack McAllister, "The Unlikely Daniel Webster Jones: First Spanish Translations from the Book of Mormon," *Ensign*, August 1981: 50.

2. Beginning in 1875 Helaman Pratt served a series of proselyting and exploration missions in Mexico. Later, he was called on a life's mission to the colonies in Chihuahua. http://helaman.pratt-family.org.

3. Latter-day Saint missionaries also carried the gospel to the Navajos, the Pueblos, and the Zunis living in Arizona and New Mexico. Ammon Tenney assisted in baptizing more than one hundred Zuni Indians. *Our Heritage: A Brief History of The Church of Jesus Christ of Latter-day Saints* (Salt Lake City: The Church of Jesus Christ of Latter-day Saints, 1996), 93–95.

4. *Stalwarts South of the Border*, eds. Nelle Spilsbury Hatch and B. Carmon Hardy (El Paso: Texas Western College Press, 1985), 543–52.

5. Agricol Lozano Herrera, *Historia del Mormonismo en Mexico* (Mexico City: Editorial Zarahemla, 1983), 12–14.

6. McAllister, "The Unlikely Daniel Webster," 50.

Beginning the Work in Mexico 29

7. Joseph Fielding Smith, *Essentials in Church History* (Salt Lake City: Deseret Books, 1950), 634–35.

8. When Francisco Madero launched his revolution, nearly 4,500 Anglo-Mormons lived in eight colonies in Chihuahua and Sonora. Nearly 10 percent of all Americans in Mexico were Mormons. Craig Livingston, "'They Are Our Brothers': High Mormon Officials Respond to the Mexican Revolution, 1910–1917" (M.A. thesis, Princeton University, 1999), ii.

9. Mormons established permanent colonies in Mexico at the direction of President John Taylor for the purpose of finding a place where the Saints could live peacefully while practicing polygamy without interference by the government. In 1895, Anthony Ivins was appointed to act as president of a stake that was to be organized in Mexico. It should be understood that he had the authority to perform marriage ceremonies for "time and eternity" which were not required to be performed in a temple due to the great distance of Mexico from the nearest temple. From 1896 to 1908, Brother Ivins would frequently be visited by a couple from the U.S. having a letter from the Presidency instructing him to marry them. A record of each of these marriages was meticulously recorded by Brother Ivins. Over the course of those years seven ceremonies were performed in 1897, ten in 1898, six in 1899 (one of these ceremonies is recorded as being performed by A. O. Woodruff, member of the Quorum of the Twelve and son of President Wilford Woodruff), two in 1900, two in 1901, nine in 1902, eleven in 1903, and five in 1904 (prior to the Smith manifesto). It was never understood by the Mormons in Mexico that the Woodruff manifesto of September 1890 in any manner prohibited the practice of polygamy by Church members residing outside the United States. His statement, "I hereby declare my intention to submit to those laws, and to use my influence with the members of the Church over which I preside to have them do likewise.... And I now publicly declare that my advice to the Latter-day Saints is to refrain from contracting any marriage forbidden by the law of the land" was understood to have no bearing on plural marriages contracted in countries where no law prohibited the practice. H. Grant Ivins, "Polygamy in Mexico as Practiced by the Mormon Church, 1895–1905," Heber Grant Ivins Papers, 1910–74, pp. 3–4, Utah State Historical Society, Salt Lake City.

10. Brigham H. Roberts, *Comprehensive History of the Church of Jesus Christ of Latter-day Saints*, 6 vols. (Salt Lake City: Deseret Book Company, 1954), 4:413.

11. Moses Thatcher and two others organized the first branch of the Church in Mexico City on November 13, 1879, with Dr. Plotino C. Rhodacanaty as the branch president. *Our Heritage*, 93.

12. "Hugo (Salvioli) and I translated the Book of Abraham while I

was serving in La Plata during 1948. It ran in the *Mensajero Deseret*. I don't remember if it was serialized or ran in one issue. We also translated about two thirds of William E. Barrett's *The History of the Church*, which did run monthly in the *Mensajero Deseret*.

"We also translated *The Greatest Thing in the World* by Henry Drummond. When I was MTC President in Santiago, Chile—1990–92, Hugo and I went over it again, and I printed seven hundred copies. Hugo took three hundred and I took the rest and gave a copy to each of the missionaries who went through our MTC.

"In ... 1995, my wife and I translated Duane Crowther's *Prophecy, Key to the Future* into Spanish. It was published both by Horizon Publishers and by a company in Mexico." H. Clay Gorton, e-mail to translator Erin Jennings, September 27, 2005.

13. Eduardo Balderas, "Northward to Mesa," *Ensign* (September 1972): 30.

Chapter 3

THE SOUTH AMERICA MISSION

Upon the return of Rufus Allen, Parley P. Pratt, and his wife Phoebe to the United States, seventy-six years would pass before the preaching of the gospel was reinstated in South America.

With the *Libro de Mormón*, *Trozos Selectos de Doctrina y Covenios*, a few hymns,[1] and *El Evangelio Restaurado* pamphlets, the way had finally been paved for proselytizing work to begin.

South Americans were inspired to promulgate laws that extended religious freedom. Thus, the Church was accepted and recognized legally in those countries where its work had begun.

Joseph Smith believed that the Promised Land stretched across all of the Americas. It was the land in which Lehi arrived and where millions of his descendants still reside. According to the Book of Mormon, amazing histories occurred on this ground. Numerous archaeological findings valued by the Latter-day Saints are considered by some to be additional evidence of the veracity of the Book of Mormon.

Melvin J. Ballard of the Quorum of the Twelve.

The Missionaries Arrive in South America

In 1923, two significant Latter-day Saint families emigrated from Germany to Argentina, the Friedrichs and Hoppe families. After a while, they wrote to the First Presidency requesting that missionaries be assigned to the country.

On September 3, 1925 it was announced that the First Presidency was considering the possibility of opening a mission in South America. Later that year, at the October semiannual general conference, Melvin J. Ballard of the Quorum of the Twelve, announced that he, along with Rulon S. Wells and Rey L. Pratt, had been chosen for the task of opening the South America Mission.

Elders Ballard, Wells, and Pratt telegraphed the First Presidency with the news of their arrival in Buenos Aires. Shortly thereafter they registered in the office of the American consulate.

The First Converts in South America

In his history journal of the South America Mission, Rey L. Pratt recorded the following:

> December 6, 1925: The boat docked at the harbor of Buenos Aires, North Basin at seven in the morning, after a voyage of over seven thousand miles according to the ship's log, in most pleasant weather without a moment's sea sickness for either of the brethren.
>
> They were met at the dock by Brothers Wilhelm Friedrichs, Emil Hoppe, their wives, and several friends they had interested in the gospel, who welcomed them.
>
> The brethren took quarters at the Grand Hotel the first night, but were taken to Brother Friedrich's home in the Liniers section of the city where they had lunch, and at four p.m. attended a cottage meeting at the home of Ernst Biébersdorf, Irala 1830, Dock Sud, Buenos Aires, Argentina, this being the first meeting held by the brethren in South America.

Rulon S. Wells and Melvin J. Ballard standing in Parque Tres de Febrero in Buenos Aires. The picture was most likely taken on the day of dedication.

In 1997 Sister María M. Biébersdorf-Párraga related the following:

> During World War I (1914–18), my parents decided to move to Argentina, where my aunt Anna Kullick lived. At that time there was work in Argentina and the situation in Germany was very difficult.
>
> Father, mother, and I arrived in Argentina on April 3, 1923, and rented the house at Irala 1830, Dock Sud. My memories of that house were that it was made of wood veneer and was built on stilts because of the frequent flooding in the area.
>
> Before the arrival of the missionaries, Hoppe and Friedrichs gave my father a Book of Mormon. When my father took the Book of Mormon, he read it, felt it was the true Church, and soon wanted to be baptized.

The first group of Saints in South America. Standing: (from left to right) Rulon S. Wells, Wilhelm Friedrichs, Jacob Kullick, Emil Hoppe, Herta Kullick, Ernst Biébersdorf, María Cziesla-Biébersdorf, and Melvin J. Ballard. Seated, left: Anna Biébersdorf-Kullick, Hildegard Hoppe, and Elisa Plassman. Seated on laps: Edith Elisabeth Biébersdorf and María M. Biébersdorf. Standing front, left: Sophia Hoppe, Minna Fredericke-Friedrichs

The South America Mission   35

María M. Biébersdorf-Párraga and Edith Elisabeth Biébersdorf-Lencina (1997) seventy-two years after the missionaries arrived at Dock Sud. These two faithful sisters are the two children that appear seated on the second row in the previous photo.

I was a small girl but knew Elder Ballard was a very friendly person. Elder Rulon S. Wells blessed me.

Papa told me that Elder Ballard was a messenger of God, that the Church was true, and that Elder Ballard had the authority to preach the gospel on this earth.

Elder Ballard visited our house frequently in Dock Sud. In his conversations, my father would often mention the things he had learned from their preaching.[2]

On Saturday, December 12, 1925, on the banks of the Rio de la Plata, Melvin J. Ballard baptized Jacob and Anna Kullick, their daughter Herta Kullick, and Ernst and María Biébersdorf.[3] All were confirmed on the following day at the Kullick family's home in Lanús. This became the location of the first sacrament and confirmation meeting in the South America Mission.

The Dedication of South America

On Christmas Day 1925, Elders Ballard, Wells, and Pratt arrived at Parque Tres de Febrero, Buenos Aires. In a small grove of weeping willows near the banks of the Rio de la Plata,[4] Elder Ballard offered a prayer dedicating South America for the preaching of the Gospel. He then gave thanks for having the opportunity to be present and pronounced his blessing:

> Bless the presidents, governors, and leading officials of these American countries, that they may kindly receive us, and give us permission to open the doors of salvation, to the people of these lands. May they be blessed in administering the affairs of their several offices, that great good may come unto the people and that peace may be upon these nations that Thou has made free, through Thy blessings upon the valiant liberators of these lands, that righteousness may obtain, and full liberty for the preaching of Thy gospel prevail. Stay the power of evil that it shall not triumph over Thy work, but that all Thine enemies shall be subdued, and Thy truth be triumphant.
>
> And now, O Father, by authority of the blessing and appointment, of thy servant, the president of the Church, and by the authority of the holy apostleship, which I hold, I do turn the key, unlock and open the door, for the preaching of the gospel, in all these South American nations; and do rebuke, and command to be stayed, every power that would oppose the preaching of the gospel, in these lands. And we do bless, and dedicate these nations and this land, for the preaching of the gospel. And we do all this, that salvation may come, to all men and that Thy name may be honored and glorified, in this part of the Land of Zion.[5]

After singing the hymn "Loor al Profeta"[6] they enjoyed the glorious spirit of Elder Ballard and listened to each of the elders speak of their missions and of their perfect love for each other and for the work of the Lord.

The South America Mission 37

Parque Tres de Febrero (July 1926). Left: Reinhold and Ella Stoof, Melvin J. Ballard, Rey L. Pratt, and J. Vernon Sharp.

The missionary group. Seated far right is Reinhold Stoof.

Elder Ballard then said that many Europeans would hear the gospel in this land, but that our work would focus mainly on the South American people.[7] The emotion felt by this statement brought many to tears.

Unfortunately, serious health problems plagued Rulon S. Wells and he was forced to return to the United States. Elders Ballard and Pratt diligently continued their mission work of teaching new missionaries until the Presidency instructed them to return to Salt Lake City.

In a testimony meeting in Buenos Aires with the German Saints held July 4, 1926, Elder Ballard pronounced the following prophetic declaration:

> The work of the Lord will grow slowly for a time here just as an oak grows slowly from an acorn. It will not shoot up in a day as does the sunflower that grows quickly then dies. But thousands will join the Church here. It will be divided into more than one mission and will be one of the strongest in the Church. The work here is the smallest that it will ever be. The day will come when the Lamanites in this land will be given a chance. The South America Mission will be a power in the Church.[8]

The Second Group of Missionaries

On June 6, 1926, J. Vernon Sharp and Waldo I. Stoddard arrived in Buenos Aires. When Elder Ballard began looking for the new missionaries, he found them gathering with the German Saints and a few Argentine investigators at a meeting coordinated by Rey L. Pratt. In the meeting, Elder Sharp's Spanish would be translated by Elder Pratt into English so that President Stoof, who did not speak Spanish, could then translate it into German. However, when Elder Sharp began to speak, Elder Stoof said that he could understand each word perfectly. When the address was finished, President Stoof translated every word into German. It has since been frequently retold, how Elder Stoof was able to enjoy the gift of languages up to his last days.⁹

Elder Melvin J. Ballard

Older members of the Church in Buenos Aires still continue to recount stories of Elder Ballard, mentioning his excellent qualities of dignity, respect, and brotherly love.

Since the mission work required a great deal of walking the streets of Buenos Aires and distributing the pamphlets *El Evangelio Restaurado*, the work proved to be very strenuous. The line of streetcars that united Liniers with the central zone was one of the more frequented places. Proselytizing in the streets was alternated with meetings at Rivadavia 8972 or in homes of German members in Liniers, Dock Sud, and Lanús. The first missionaries worked among modest, simple people and quickly gained their confidence and respect.

After returning from his mission in South America, Elder Ballard reported the following at general conference:

> At first it was very difficult to find complete satisfaction while preaching the gospel in a country where I had no knowledge of the native language. But, after a while, I learned to read and speak the language. I was very fulfilled when partnering with Brother Pratt. We invited people to attend our meetings and Elder Pratt would convey my testimony to them in Spanish. I was able to visit 12,500 homes, handing out our printed message and inviting people to our meetings. We held 234 meetings, which kept Brother Pratt very busy preaching.
>
> During this time we found ourselves doing the same things that we did when we first began our work as missionaries. When we traveled we always did so without purse or scrip. However, we found that it was more difficult now than in past years to allocate our time.¹⁰

Reinhold and Ella Stoof with their children.

EVANGELIO RESTAURADO

Conferencias todos los Domingos a las 19.30 horas

RIVADAVIA 8972

Por los recien llegados misioneros de Norte América

— DE LA —

Iglesia de Jesu Cristo de los Santos de los Ultimos Días

— SOBRE LA —

RESTAURACION DE NUEVO A LA TIERRA DEL EVANGELIO DE CRISTO Y EL RESTABLECIMIENTO DE SU IGLESIA

El público cordialmente invitado.   ENTRADA GRATIS.

Con el fin de establecer una misión evangélica en Buenos Aires, recientemente han llegado a esta ciudad misioneros y altos funcionarios y oficiales de la IGLESIA DE JESUCRISTO DE LOS SANTOS DE LOS ULTIMOS DIAS.

En la calle de Rivadavia N.° 8972 celebran sus cultos y servicios religiosos, y respetuosamente invitan al honorable público de Buenos Aires. Los cultos y servicios se verificarán todos los días domingos a las 19.30 horas.

No se trata simplemente de una misión protestante, pues la Iglesia de Jesucristo de los Santos de los Ultimos Días, comúnmente llamada "Mormona", no es una iglesia protestante, sino que es la Iglesia de nuestro Señor Jesucristo restablecida en su pureza, con la misma organización de apóstoles y profetas, con los mismos dones y poderes que existieron en la Iglesia de Cristo cuando El anduvo con los hombres sobre la tierra. El Evangelio que predican en esta Iglesia es también el Evangelio puro de Cristo; restaurado de nuevo a la tierra en estos últimos días, de acuerdo con las palabras del Apóstol Juan en su Revelación, capítulo 14 y versículos 6 y 7: "Y vi otro ángel volar por en medio del cielo, que tenía el evangelio eterno, para que evangelizase a los que moran en la tierra, y a toda nación, y tribu, y lengua, y pueblo, Diciendo a alta voz: Temed a Dios, y dadle gloria; porque la hora de su juicio es venida; y adorad al que ha hecho el cielo, y la tierra, y la mar, y las fuentes de las aguas".

¿QUE, PUES, ES ESTA IGLESIA?

En primer lugar diremos lo que no es. El "Mormonismo" no es una religión nueva. No es un evangelio nuevo. No presenta nuevos ni extraños dioses. No predica a otro Cristo ni aboga a otro Redentor para el hombre, sino Jesús de Nazaret. No presenta ningún plan nuevo de salvación para los hombres. No introduce ningunas ordenanzas nuevas que tienen que ser observadas, ningunos símbolos nuevos en lugar de las realidades de la gracia y el poder. No enseña ningunos nuevos técnicos de intimidad con Dios y con Cristo y con el Espíritu Santo. No recomienda ningún sacerdocio nuevo como un medio de autoridad divina para hacer cosas sagradas o administrar en ordenanzas santas. No enseña ningún otro código, sino la ley moral del Evangelio de Cristo. No hace otro resumen de la ley de los profetas sino que "Amarás al Señor tu Dios de todo tu corazón, de toda tu alma, y de toda tu mente:... Amarás a tu prójimo como a ti mismo". No substituye nada por los Diez Mandamientos ni por el Sermón en el Monte.

El "Mormonismo" es simplemente una nueva dispensación de la Religión Antigua; del antiguo, el primero, y el único Evangelio, "El Evangelio Eterno" de Jesucristo, con todo lo que es asociado con él, y que le pertenece. Si reclamara ser una religión nueva, un evangelio nuevo, entonces los hombres pronto pudieran disponer de él; pudieran saber que no puede ser verdadero, porque hay tan solamente una sola religión. "Un Señor, una Fe, un Bautismo, un Dios y Padre de todos". No hay más avangelio que uno: "No hay otro nombre debajo del cielo, dado a los hombres, en que nos sea necesario ser salvos". (Actos 4:12); "Mas si nosotros, o un ángel del cielo os anunciare otro evangelio... sea maldito. (Gálatas 1:8). El "Mormonismo" reclama ser, tan solamente, Una Nueva Dispensación del Uno y Único Evangelio.

¿HA HABIDO UNA NECESIDAD DE UNA RESTAURACION?

En vista de la apostasía predicha por los profetas de Dios que han dejado sus testimonios en las Sagradas Escrituras, y el hecho del cumplimiento de estas profecías entre los hombres, tenemos que confesar que si. He aquí, lo que dice Isaías: "Destruyóse, cayó la tierra: enfermó, cayó el mundo; enfermaron los altos pueblos de la tierra. Y la tierra fué mentirosa debajo de sus moradores; PORQUE TRASPASARON LAS LEYES, FALSEARON EL DERECHO, ROMPIERON EL PACTO SEMPITERNO. Por esta causa el quebrantamiento del juramento consumió a la tierra, y sus moradores fueron asolados, por esta causa fueron consumidos los moradores de la tierra, y los hombres se apocaron". (Isaías 24,4-6).

Al reflexionar por un momento se puede ver que esta profecía no tuvo su cumplimiento en el mundo

Twenty-five hundred copies of *El Evangelio Restaurado* were distributed by missionaries in the streets of Buenos Aires during Melvin J. Ballard's presidency.

The Gianfelice Family

Antonino Gianfelice was just a boy when the missionaries visited his home in 1926. After sixty-four years he recalls his first contact with the Church in these words:

> The year was 1926. My father had arrived from Italy in September 1920 with the rest of the family arriving in 1923. We made our home in Liniers. At that time I was five years old. One Sunday morning we went to visit a family friend of my father. While we were there we heard singing that sounded similar to that which is heard in church. It was coming from a nearby home. My mother asked my father to find out if it were possible for us to attend. Later that week, while distributing pamphlets door to door, Elder Friedrichs stopped by our house. The pamphlet was called *El Evangelio Restaurado* and we were told that meetings were held at Rivadavia 8972. The family we had visited began to attend Church and so we also began attending shortly thereafter.[11]

President Frederick S. Williams relates the following history of Donato Gianfelice, father of Antonino:

> The winter (June, July, and August) of 1928 was one of the wettest on record. Rain fell almost continuously for twenty-one days and the sun disappeared altogether. Buenos Aires was as flat as a tabletop and at that time had no storm drains. After a few days, the water became so deep that it was impossible for the streetcars to move and they had to stop operating. Soon all traffic had stopped. Often we waded across intersections in water up to our belts; we were always cold and wet.
> One Sunday during this period, we had to walk the sixty-five blocks to Liniers and the Gianfelice family walked back to our apartment to spend Sunday evening with us. After all the members had gone home that night, and as we missionaries were slowly gathering enough nerve to go to bed (it was very

cold), we heard a knock at the door. We wondered who in the world would be calling on us at that time on a cold and rainy winter night. It was Brother Gianfelice, who had only left an hour or so before. He said, "Will you pray to the Lord to forgive me?" "What have you done?" we asked. He explained, "When I paid my tithing this afternoon, I miscalculated and underpaid the Lord twenty centavos" (at that time about a nickel in American money). "I've come to pay the twenty centavos." "Why in the world did you walk all those sixty-five blocks in the rain when you knew we would be in your home on Tuesday for Mutual, and you could have paid your tithing at that time?" He said, "I would not have been able to sleep knowing that I had cheated the Lord in my tithing." He paid it and then walked home.

The following week he brought the envelope with his earnings (he was paid in cash) and he asked me, "Will you do me a favor and please take out my tithing so that I don't forget?" I answered him, "No, no, you must do it. Tithing is a matter between you and the Lord; you ought to be the one to pay to the Lord what you owe to the Lord."[12]

The Gianfelice family in ca. 1940.

Left: Nicolas Lafrata, Domingo Cuicci, Donato Gianfelice, Waldo I. Stoddard (behind Gianfelice), J. Vernon Sharp, Emilia Notaro de Gianfelice with two of their children, Antonino and Juana Gianfelice.

Left: Heber M. Clegg, Luigi Notaro, Antonino Gianfelice, and María Antonia Notaro at the baptism of Antonino Gianfelice in 1928.

The Presidency of Reinhold Stoof (1926–35)

After the mission of Melvin J. Ballard and Rey L. Pratt, the Church continued to grow at a slow but constant rate.

For nine years Reinhold Stoof had presided over the South America Mission. At that time the work was mainly carried out in the German community of Buenos Aires. The first missionaries who served in Argentina are:

NAME	AGE	ORIGIN	ARRIVAL
J. Vernon Sharp	20	Salt Lake City, Utah	6/6/26
Waldo I. Stoddard	21	Baker, Oregon	6/6/26
Lewis E. Christian	24	St. George, Utah	12/22/26
I. Russell Spencer	21	Centerville, Utah	12/22/26
Preston E. Ashton	20	Salt Lake City, Utah	12/22/26
Heber M. Clegg	19	Salt Lake City, Utah	12/22/26
Jewel C. Jensen	19	Bear River, Utah	12/22/26
Douglas B. Merrill	27	Duncan, Arizona	3/2/27
William Fred Heinz	19	Rexburg, Idaho	3/2/27
Paul W. Davis	19	Phoenix, Arizona	3/2/27
Frederick S. Williams	18	Phoenix, Arizona	3/2/27
Harry P. Brundage	26	Ray, Arizona	10/9/27
Emil Schindler	23	Germany	10/9/27
John B. Gardner	22	Salt Lake City, Utah	4/26/29
Victor Wheeler	20	Ogden, Utah	4/26/29

President Stoof lived in Salt Lake City but he was originally from Germany. He was a man with great discipline and an entrepreneurial spirit. He was greatly respected by members and missionaries alike, standing as an example with his firm leadership style and independence.

On one occasion, he and his family were living on very limited resources. The German members realized that the family was in need of basic necessities and decided to write to the First

Reinhold Stoof, president of the South America Mission (1926--35).

Presidency to ask for monetary help for them. Sometime later, President Stoof realized what the members had done and severely reprimanded them for asking for the help.

The Gospel and the Lamanites

Ever since the Book of Mormon was given to the Prophet Joseph Smith, the preaching of the gospel to the Lamanites has been an important subject for the leaders of the Church.

When the South America Mission was opened, Melvin J. Ballard said in his dedication prayer:

Luacine Clark, J. Reuben Clark, Ella Stoof, and Reinhold Stoof, with missionaries and members in Buenos Aires (1933).

> We are thankful that we are the bearer, of these glad tidings, to the peoples of the South American nations.
> We also pray that we may see the beginning of the fulfillment of the promises contained in the Book of Mormon to the Indians of this land, who are descendents of Lehi, millions of whom reside in this country.[13]

Even though the preaching of the gospel was directed toward the German immigrants, President Stoof felt a great urgency to take the gospel to those native of Argentina.[14] In March 1927, Douglas B. Merrill and Lewis E. Christian, accompanied by J. Vernon Sharp, who was returning to the United States via Bolivia and Peru, were sent to the province of Jujuy, at the north end of Argentina, on the border of Bolivia. The missionaries remained there working for about a month but soon had to return to Buenos Aires due to difficulties of preaching and the proliferation of disease.[15] Lewis E. Christian wrote the following:

> We tried for days to get a start in this new city. At first the people were friendly and enthusiastic about our message but they soon would have nothing to do with us. The Catholic priests have told them that they will go to hell if they even talked to us. We can't get lodging or food or even a conversation with anyone. During these discouraging days I had a most disturbing dream in which it was indicated to me that something is terribly wrong back home.[16]

In March 1927, President Stoof, accompanied by Waldo I. Stoddard, traveled to Chaco to find out if the people there were more receptive than those in northern Argentina. Eight days later they returned to Buenos Aires with the conclusion that the conditions were not yet favorable enough to initiate preaching in those areas.

German members of the White Branch in Buenos Aires, 1938.

The Lanús Sunday School at the Biébersdorf home, 1937.

Eric Karl Fischer, baptized as a teenager in 1936 in Ballester, was one of the first German members. Living in the Mercedes Branch, Buenos Aires, he was a true pioneer of the Church from the time of his baptism.

The first mission presidents assumed at that time that the Lamanites were those groups that lived in primitive conditions in remote areas of the country.

The work with these groups was challenging, but the leaders understood that it was necessary for the Church to reach greater numbers in the country very soon in order to produce true spiritual and cultural change. Because of the unfavorable conditions, the efforts among these groups ceased.

At the same time they began to find the descendants of Lehi, the Lamanites, were also in the cities and towns. The blood relations of Lehi were extensively scattered among the population.

The Creoles, that is to say, the children of Europeans born in America mixed with the children of Lehi, constitute the majority of the Argentinean population.[17]

The gospel had successfully circled all of Argentina. The Lamanites, immigrants, and Creoles accepted the gospel and all were converted to "the people of Zion," the "lineage of Israel"; the prophesies of the Book of Mormon had been realized.

The time had come in the Church where the numbers had reached a sufficient level in Argentina and in other countries of South America to bless the forgotten Lamanites and those who were wandering in the desert, fulfilling the 1926 declaration of Melvin J. Ballard:

> ... but the day will come when the Lamanites of this earth will have the opportunity."[18]

Even though the missionaries were frustrated in their efforts with the Argentines, this did not discourage President Stoof. By the end of 1927 he had plans to visit Brazil and investigate the possibility of initiating work there.

The Visit of Elder J. Reuben Clark

In 1933, J. Reuben Clark of the First Presidency, visited Buenos Aires. He then visited Montevideo as a former delegate from the United States. During his short visit he presented a message to the brothers in the Liniers Branch while instructing the elders about a special mission.

Elder Clark was the first General Authority of the Church to visit Argentina after Elder Ballard's mission.

The Mission of Reinhold Stoof Ends

In 1935, after devoting and sacrificing nine years to the South America Mission, President Reinhold Stoof returned to the United States.

At the general conference in April 1936, he reported on his mission to South America. At the conclusion of his speech in the tabernacle, he stated the following:

> There are great harvests awaiting the Church in South America. I have no doubts in my mind about this. God has granted me a testimony on this. I pray in the name of Jesus Christ that God continues to bless South America.[19]

The Church in Rosario

Sometime between October 24–28, 1928, the first missionaries, Heber M. Clegg and Frederick S. Williams, arrived in Rosario.

The missionaries traveled by train from Buenos Aires. When arriving in Rosario, they began looking for members of the Church who lived in the city. They found a couple from Switzerland who were members of the Church before they emigrated.

The South America Mission   53

They also found a German member living in Los Delicias. On Sunday morning they attended a Pentecostal service and handed out pamphlets, returning that afternoon to Buenos Aires on an oldsteam ship. This was the way the gospel first arrived in Rosario.

Two years later permanent work began. On November 13, 1930, Reinhold Stoof from the South America Mission arrived accompanied by Victor Wheeler of Utah and Lothaire A. Bluth of Mexico. In that day, the city had a population of almost one million people. Exactly eight days after the arrival of the missionaries, a site was rented two blocks from the present Echesortu Chapel.

Permission was obtained from the municipal authorities, and on December 14 the city dedicated for the preaching of the gospel.

The First Baptisms

The first baptisms took place February 6, 1932, in the waters of the Arroyo Saladillo. The missionaries baptized María Catalina Paz-Arias and her daughter Ramona Benita Arias-Gavioli. They also performed the marriage of Juan José Caminos to María Ducher.

They continued the work and in 1939 the Rosario Centro Branch was organized, which, at that time, happened to be called Echesortu. Also, the Sorrento Branch was organized with four missionaries in a small hall at the corner of Cortada 33 (now Arroyito) and Almafuerte. This branch, now in the Rosario North Stake began with a group of pioneering families headed by Sister Dorinda Prieto and her children Hilda, Angel, and Manuel, who were baptized on December 10, 1936.

On February 16–18, 1940, the new Sorrento Branch mission house at Gurruchaga 967 played host to an important meeting. It was at this time that the welfare plan was instituted.

Here, the missionaries served as branch presidents, taught the Relief Society, directed music, and gave talks. There was only one organ to share between the different locations. At the end of each branch meeting they would load the organ into a *mateo* (a cart with two wheels drawn by horses) and quickly transport it to another location so that there would be organ music for their meetings.

In those days good speakers were not abundant. The missionaries would travel by streetcar back and forth between the Echesortu and Salta Avenue branches. These were heroic moments in the growth of the Church.[20]

Notes

1. The Spanish hymnal, *Himnos de la Iglesia de los Santos de los Últimas Días*, currently contains 209 Spanish hymns as compared to the English version which contains 341. Not only are there English hymns that do not have Spanish equivalents, but there are also Spanish hymns that do not have English counterparts. "The Song of the Heart," *New Era,* August 2003, 36.
2. María M. Biébersdorf-Párraga, Oral History, 1997.
3. The first converts were foreigners. Women outnumbered men two to one. From the first baptismal service, the German image of the Mormon Church and the predominance of women became two constant problems with which the church struggled in Argentina. Michael B. Smurthwaite, "Socio-Political Factors Affecting the Growth of the Mormon Church in Argentina Since 1925" (M.A. thesis, Brigham Young University, 1968), 10.
4. Gerry Spencer, "Dedication of South America for Gospel Commemorated," *Church News,* December 5, 2000. http://www.mormons today.com/001208/N6SouthAmDedication01.shtml.
5. Melvin J. Ballard, "Dedication Prayer on South America," December 25, 1925, South American Mission History, December 6, 1925–February 26, 1926, vol. II, History Division, LDS Chruch Archives, Salt Lake City; punctuation standardized.

The South America Mission 55

6. "Praise to the Man," currently hymn no. 27 in the English hymnal.

7. Spanish-speaking Argentines so overwhelmingly outnumbered those who spoke German at Mormon meetings it would appear that the missionaries should have turned their efforts toward that people, the German converts notwithstanding. Their failure to pursue the Spanish-speaking majority became the first major drawback. A second mistake followed the first as the first Presidency chose Reinhold Stoof who spoke only German and English to replace Ballard as mission president in 1926. Smurthwaite, "Socio-Political Factors," 10.

8. J. Vernon Sharp, Diary, quoted in *Melvin J. Ballard, Crusader for Righteousness* (Salt Lake City: Bookcraft, 1966), 84.

9. This experience makes the emphasis on German even more amazing when coupled with the fact that Rulon S. Wells had returned home due to illness in January 1926 and Wells was the only missionary who spoke German. Smurthwaite, "Socio-Political Factors," 10.

10. Hugo N. Salvioli, Oral History.

11. Antonino Gianfelice, Oral History and Manuscript 1985–86, pp. 2–3, History Division, LDS Church Archives, Buenos Aires.

12. Frederick S. and Frederick G. Williams, *From Acorn to Oak Tree: A Personal History of the Establishment and First Quarter Century Development of the South American Missions* (Fullerton: 1987), 58.

13. Ballard, "Dedication Prayer."

14. Attendance figures of the early meetings illustrated the trend toward Spanish-speaking contacts. While Ballard and Pratt proselyted in Buenos Aires, Spanish-speaking contacts outnumbered those who spoke German by over four to one. Attendance at meetings held in German remained constant, while those conducted in Spanish attracted many more hearers. South American Mission History, December 6, 1925–February 26, 1926, Vol. 2, LDS Church Archives.

15. Malaria was a constant threat to the health of the missionaries due to the numerous mosquito populations. Douglas B. Merrill contracted malaria fever and was very ill. Lewis Earl Christian, *Sandstone, Blackrock, and a Few Other Solid Matters: The Story of My Life*, (Family Book: 1979), 76.

16. Ibid.

17. In the sixteenth through eighteen centuries, a Creole was considered any white person born in Spanish America of Spanish parents, as distinguished from an American resident who had been born in Spain. http://www.britannica.com/eb/article?eu=28289.

18. Ballard, "Dedication Prayer."

19. The Church of Jesus Christ of Latter-day Saints, *Conference Report, 1936,* p. 89.

20. Manuel Sueldo, "Noticias Locales," *Liahona,* May 1998, 7.

Chapter 4

THE BRAZIL AND ARGENTINA MISSIONS

In December 1927, President Stoof, accompanied by Elder Stoddard, traveled to Brazil to visit the German colonies.[1] The missionaries arrived in the colony of Joinville where they were successful in making many contacts. President Stoof spoke to a group of approximately 142 people. In mid-January 1928 they returned to Buenos Aires with a positive impression of Brazil.[2]

In September 1928, President Stoof, accompanied by William F. Heinz and Emil Schindler, traveled to Joinville to begin work in Brazil. After they rented a house and met with several people, President Stoof and Elder Stoddard returned to Buenos Aires, leaving the other two elders to continue working in Brazil. The first baptismal service was performed on April 14, 1929. Elder Schindler baptized Bertha and Theodore Sell and Elder Heinz baptized Siegfried and Adel Sell.[3]

On February 9, 1935 the First Presidency of the Church announced that the South America Mission would be divided.[4]

The Church in Brazil

In the first years they were only able to preach to those who spoke German since there were no pamphlets or books translated into Portuguese.[5] By 1938 the missionaries had mastered the Portuguese language. An elder who spoke German was paired with one who spoke Portuguese. This made it possible for them to speak with all Brazilian people. During World War II, and continuing thereafter, the Brazilian government prohibited the use of the German language. For this reason the Brazil Mission was transformed little by little into a Portuguese-speaking mission.

On March 8, 1948, Stephen L Richards and along his wife, Irene, made the first visit by a General Authority to the Brazil Mission, providing spiritual strength and courage to the missionaries.

In March 1949 a mission home was established in São Paulo. That same year the first two missionaries arrived to the field.

In January 1954 there was a visit from President David O. McKay. He made a favorable impression with the newspaper press and government officials who met with him. Many members traveled long distances and slept on the ground outside the São Paulo Chapel just for a chance to hear the words of the Prophet.

During his visit to Río de Janeiro, President McKay climbed the steps to the famous statue Christ the Redeemer,[6] which stood more than 230 feet tall and dominated the bay. There, he spoke the well-known invitation from the Lord, "Come unto me, all *ye* that labour and are heavy laden, and I will give you rest." (Matt. 11:28). He emphasized that the statue was a tribute to the Brazilians, whose money had helped build the monument.

During his visit in 1956, Henry D. Moyle, accompanied by his wife, Clara, stated that it would take great force to awaken the spirit among the people. The missionaries were able to testify to the truthfulness of the words of Elder Moyle and earlier visiting authorities that they felt the spirit of the Lord working in them and in the people of Brazil. That year the baptisms doubled in number.[7]

In February 1959, Spencer W. Kimball visited the Brazilian Saints on his way to the Uruguay Mission. Upon his return he dedicated the Ipanema Chapel. In September of the same year, Harold B. Lee, under the direction of the First Presidency, arrived to divide the mission. Asael T. Sorensen, who was designated as the new Brazil South Mission president, accompanied him.[8]

The Argentina Mission

In 1935 the South America Mission was divided into the Brazil and Argentina Missions.[9] On August 14, W. Ernest Young arrived in Argentina with his wife, Cecile, and their three children, Amy, Walter, and Carl.

The missionaries under the direction of President Young were very dedicated to the work. The Quilmes, Rosario, Pergamino, La Plata, and San Nicolás Branches were established.[10]

The Presidency of W. Ernest Young (1935–38)

W. Ernest Young came from the Mormon colony of Chihuahua in northern Mexico. His work in Argentina emphasized the Spanish-speaking people.[11]

In September 1938, President Young made his last visits to several of the mission branches to say good-bye and to bear his testimony. On September 7 a final farewell meeting was held in the Liniers Branch with 250 members and friends gathering for the occasion. There were talks, hymns, songs, and expressions of love and brotherhood:

> This was my last chance to bear my testimony, telling the people that I had known many pioneers who knew the Prophet Joseph Smith, and that their testimonies meant much to me, men who had gone through many trials for the gospel. They had heard the testimony of the Prophet Joseph Smith and knew that he was indeed the Prophet of the last days. I thanked all who had contributed to the success of the mission.[12]

The Presidency of Frederick S. Williams (1938–42)

At President Williams's arrival, there were 438 members, with sixty-six of them being baptized that same year. There were twenty rented buildings, twenty Primary organizations, eight Relief Societies, fourteen Sunday schools, and ten Mutual Improvement Associations. There were forty-seven missionaries in the mission.

In 1938, mission influence extended to Córdoba, Bahía Blanca, Moron, and Nueva Pompeya. On January 6, 1939, the first baptismal service in the Liniers Chapel was performed.

Under the presidency of Frederick S. Williams, the Church became well-known in the country. Social and sporting activities helped the work progress.

The activities of basketball teams and musical groups helped to improve the image of the Church in some sectors of the population.

The Brazil and Argentina Missions 61

A group of Buenos Aires missionaries in 1938 with W. Ernest Young (standing in middle in the light suit).

Gerald O. Lynn at Emil Hoppe's pond on Tigre Island (1939).

Armin Hofmann, left, Luis Sghimkat, and Elder Ostendorf.

Branches and meeting houses in the Argentina Mission-1938

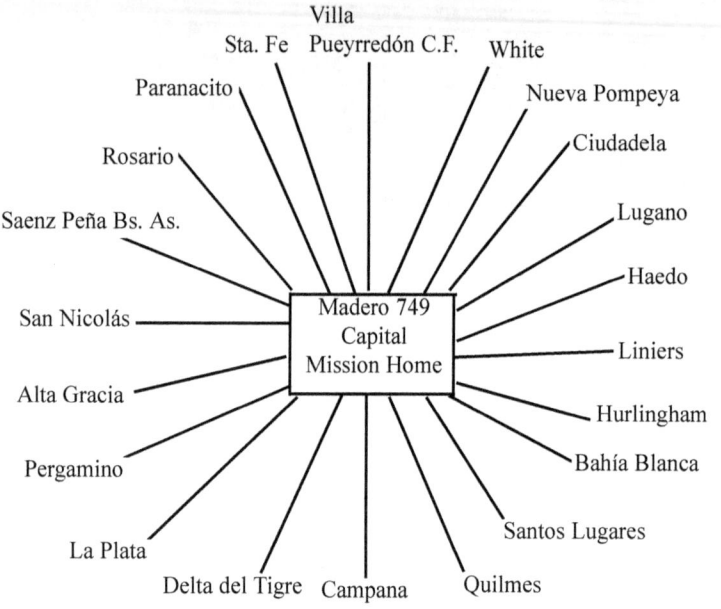

- Villa Pueyrredón C.F.
- Sta. Fe
- Paranacito
- White
- Nueva Pompeya
- Rosario
- Ciudadela
- Saenz Peña Bs. As.
- Lugano
- San Nicolás
- Haedo
- Madero 749 Capital Mission Home
- Liniers
- Alta Gracia
- Hurlingham
- Pergamino
- Bahía Blanca
- La Plata
- Santos Lugares
- Delta del Tigre
- Campana
- Quilmes

Elder Ostendorf at the baptism of a German sister. Carmen Scholz is on the right with her son Ricardo.

To join the Church at this time was a true challenge. One had to face ridicule, lack of understanding, and disgust from family and friends. It was also difficult to find serious contacts and interested investigators. They received the missionaries as a curiosity and wanted to make them their friends. However, when the doctrine of the restored gospel and baptism was preached, the missionaries were rejected.

The growth of the Church progressed very slowly. The missionaries had very little guidance in proselytizing and lacked supplies for their teaching of the scriptures.[13]

It was very common at that time for churches to preach door to door. However, people had negative thoughts of those preachers, who, in general, were seen as being a little fanatical. When the missionaries arrived, they assumed that this negative image prevailed and therefore did not visit the people. However, the people were really concerned with their own economic problems, which were very different from ours at that time. Women were very busy with their homes while men worked every day, not returning home until late at night. It was also very common for women not to let a stranger into their home if their husband were not present. At that time there were very few baptisms, with the missionaries' primary job being to distribute pamphlets.[14]

The Williams Family, Pioneers of South America

With the following words, Frederick S. Williams, remembered his arrival to Buenos Aires as a missionary seventy years earlier:

> On March 2, 1927, we arrived in Buenos Aires, my home for the next two years. The first people we met were Elders Waldo I. Stoddard, Heber M. Clegg, and Jewel C. Jensen. The streetcar fare from the mission home on Rivadavia was four American cents.

The Williams family in 1938.

The Scholz family house on Tigre Island.

I met the mission president, Reinhold Stoof, his wife, Ella, and the other missionaries already serving, Lewis E. Christian, I. Russell Spencer, and J. Vernon Sharp. The entire missionary force, until our arrival, consisted of six missionaries, eight counting the mission president and his wife. Our arrival increased the missionary force by forty percent.

We stayed at the mission home a day or two and then moved into our own quarters a half block away. The following day we picked up our trunks from the customs house and registered at the American Consulate.

The Brazil and Argentina Missions   65

Since first hearing Elder Ballard speak at the old Phoenix Ward, I had looked forward to visiting the place where the South America Mission had been dedicated. My missionary companions were as interested as I, and after satisfying the residency requirements for Argentina and obtaining adequate living quarters, we urged the longer-term missionaries to take us there.

Parques Tres de Febrero at that time was only partially improved. The north portion was still a wilderness of willow trees, underbrush, and tangled vines. As we traveled toward the park, I thought of the three men chosen to open the mission and how they must have had feelings similar to mine. I was a stranger in a strange land who had followed their path from Salt Lake City to Buenos Aires, and now I was on my way to the spot where they had turned the key for the preaching of the gospel on the South American continent, an action that had made it possible for me to serve in this distant land. In my mind, I relived the hours when my own ship had entered Buenos Aires, the rigors of going through customs for the first time, and then the joy of seeing people of my own faith as I left the port area. These three brethren accompanying me had had the same experiences only sixteen months before.[15]

Frederick S. Williams and his family were pioneers of the Church in South America. He was called as a missionary when he turned eighteen, then returned to Argentina eleven years later as mission president. In 1947 he was called to preside over the Uruguay Mission and to open Paraguay for the preaching of the gospel. Before his call he had lived in Montevideo and went on to start the first branch there, serving as the first branch president. Later his job took him to Lima, Peru, where he also served as the first branch president.

In addition to his service in the missions of South America, he worked tirelessly in the United States. Thus it was appropriate that he be the one to start the work in the Los Angeles

Frederick S. Williams (1928).

Temple. He was counselor in the Los Angeles South Stake presidency, and served as Stake patriarch and as a sealer in the temple.

In October 1991, Frederick S. Williams passed away in Mesa, Arizona. Members of the Church in South America will always remember him as a great spiritual leader, a friend with a model family, and as someone who

Frederick S. Williams at the Buenos Aires Temple dedication in 1986. When he arrived in Argentina in 1927, there were a total of eight missionaries on the entire continent. Seventy-five years later, there were four temples in operation, thousands of members and missionaries, and hundreds of stakes.

was certain that the gospel permitted the strengthening of the bonds and feelings of friendship in heaven more than in this life. Frederick S. Williams and his family were a great blessing to and a major factor in the success of the mission in Argentina and South America.

The First Chapel in Argentina

The Liniers Chapel not only served the resident members in the area, but also the entire Argentina Mission. For more than two decades it was the center of activities for the Church in that country; missionaries held meetings, twice a year mission conferences were held, and other conferences were held there. General Authorities would visit the Argentina Mission, arriving in Liniers for leadership meetings and speaking engagements.

The Liniers Chapel on Tonelero and the corner of Cañada de Gómez was a busy place, building the foundation of the Church as it is known today. Frederick S. Williams recalled

> On January 1, 1929, Harry Brundage and I were guests of Luigi Notaro for New Year's dinner in their new home on Tonelero Street, near the corner of Cañada de Gómez in Liniers. Luigi had just retired from the railroad and they had moved into their new quarters; there was no furniture. Sister Notaro cooked dinner on a Primus stove brought from their former home, and we ate sitting on the floor.
>
> Two years later on July 28, 1931, the Notaros transferred this same property to the Church with the understanding that they could remain in the house as long as they both lived. Their small one-story house sat back away from the street, so the Church erected the first Liniers Chapel in front, at sidewalk level. Construction began September 8, 1931 and President Stoof offered the dedication prayer November 15. This chapel served not only the needs of the Liniers Branch, but was the

building Presidents Stoof, Young, and I (for a time) used for all our mission conferences.

We soon realized that the Liniers Chapel could not meet the Saints' needs and we made plans for a larger meetinghouse to be constructed. In March 1936, President Young purchased the lot between the Notaro property and Cañada de Gómez Street. President Stoof had begun negotiating for the property in 1931.

When I arrived in the mission, the chapel was still under construction. Progress was very slow, but eventually we got the roof on and finished a second story apartment for the Notaros to replace their home, which was to be converted into classrooms.

This was something new in South America: a large chapel built and owned by the Church. Neither the Brazilian meeting house in Joinville or the first Liniers Chapel could compare in magnitude or impact. Thirteen years after the organization of the South America Mission, we had a chapel almost large enough to seat all the baptized members in Argentina...

The dedication service was held in conjunction with the April conference in the Argentina Mission. Songs were translated into Spanish for this occasion. Scheduled to perform was the mission choir directed by Ernest J. Wilkins, a girls' triple trio, and a twelve-voice missionary chorus, both organized and directed by Corraine. Among the speakers were Donato Gianfelice and Roland G. Kaiser.[16]

Miguel Angel Avila remembered:

The chapel was constructed in a very simple style, comparatively different from the way they would later be built in this country.

Large windows stretched a distance of five and a half feet from the floor. There was a platform beneath which was a white tiled baptismal font with stairs. It had two very sturdy covers, which when closed, became the floor. A simple pulpit

The Liniers Chapel under construction, 1938. Photo by Gerald O. Lynn.

The Liniers Chapel during a Sunday service. The building to the right was the old meeting place donated by the Notaro family in 1929.

was placed on the center of the lid of the baptismal font. It also had a platform with railings and a tier for the choir.[17]

At the dedication of the Liniers Chapel, President Williams stated:

> We should be thankful for the privilege of being able to live at a time in which thy promises to the Lamanites and to the house of Israel are beginning to be fulfilled; for the opportunity that we have by doing thy work and bringing souls to you; for the honor that we have of being called thyservants and thy children. We thank thee for this chapel. We thank thee for our forefathers who sacrificed everything for the gospel. Thank thee for thy Prophet Heber J. Grant, the Twelve Apostles, and the other authorities of the Church.
>
> Now, Father, we offer this house to thee. We request thy blessings on it, and as thy servant, I bless it. I dedicate and set it apart to the glory of thy name. I bless it in its entirety, from the roof to the foundation, so that it remains firm against the power of the elements, allowing nothing to disturb it, and standing here to bless many people.[18]

The First Argentine Missionaries

During the first thirty years, the Church was sustained and continued to grow, being preserved by the effort, work, and direction of the missionaries. The majority came from the central stakes of the Church and not only taught the doctrine but also the priesthood, experiences, traditions, and culture of the Latter-day Saints. These missionaries were examples of the restored gospel.

The Brazil and Argentina Missions 71

Left: Samuel Boren and Lyman Shreeve.

Left: Antonino Gianfelice and R. G. Brewer.

In the 1940s, under the direction of Argentina Mission President Frederick S. Williams, the first local missionaries were called. They were:

Luis Constantini: Liniers Branch, served from April 19, 1939 to May 25, 1940.
Samuel Boren: Haedo Branch, served from June 10, 1939 to April 9, 1940.
Salvador Parisi: Pergamino Branch, served from August 31, 1939 to April 9, 1940.
Roberto Pedro Antonietti: Haedo Branch, served from January 18, 1940 to January 9, 1941.
José Pedro Alvarez: Haedo Branch, served from January 22, 1940 to January 31, 1941.
Antonino Gianfelice: Liniers Branch, served from April 14, 1942 to July 1, 1943.[19]

Serving as a missionary was a tremendous experience in the life and preparation of these brothers. To a large extent all of them contributed to the establishment of the foundation of the Church in Argentina and South America.

In 1987, after more than forty years serving the Church, Samuel Boren stated "My Mission has been an inspiration for all my life; never will I be able to express all my gratitude." After completing his mission in 1940, Boren served in the following positions: La Plata Branch president, counselor in the Argentina Mission presidency, stake missionary, twice a temple worker in Mesa, Arizona, treasurer for the construction in South America, counselor in the Uruguay Mission presidency, A. Theodore Tuttle's assistant while he was president of the Montevideo, Mexico-Veracruz Mission, regional representative, Italy Milan Mission president, Italy Catania Mission president, and president of the Lima Peru Temple.

Roberto Pedro Antonietti, Merlo, Buenos Aires Stake Patriarch, 1999. He was one of the first missionaries to serve in Mendoza in the 1940s.

Roberto Pedro Antonietti continued serving the Church in the years following his mission. He was a counselor in the Liniers Branch presidency, Florida Branch president, counselor in the Central District, Haedo Branch president, District Mission president, member of the Argentina Mission Advisory Council, a local missionary, high priests group leader, member of the Merlo Stake High Council, bishop of Parque San Martín Ward, and Merlo Stake patriarch. He recalled his mission in Mendoza in the 1940s:

> Mission work in Mendoza consisted mainly of the distribution of pamphlets. There were many conversations at the doors of houses, and sometimes they would allow the missionaries to come inside. The people were very friendly. Little by little they managed to teach several families, with two of them being the Saldívar and Cano families. It was in the home of the Cano family that the official meetings of The Church of Jesus Christ of Latter-day Saints in the province of Mendoza began. Time had shown that Mendoza was a fertile field for the Church. As I left on the train to return and watched the landscape move farther away. I prayed fervently that God would deeply touch the hearts of the good people so that they would accept the gospel and the work there would continue to grow.[20]

José Pedro Alvarez, who served in Santa Fe, commented:

> In those days, mission work was very challenging. It was very difficult to hold gospel conversations. One day, my companion fell ill. I was reading the Book of Mormon and suddenly an impulse came over me to leave immediately and go out to distribute pamphlets. So I did. God guided me to a home where I was able to explain the gospel principles to the family. They made the decision to listen and soon wished to be baptized. That brought me great joy.

Antonino Gianfelice and companion R. G. Brewer.

Luis Constantini and his wife (left)

My call as a missionary was of great value in my life. It increased my faith and love toward my fellow man. My testimony was greatly strengthened, and this allowed me to accept the appointments and calls that God later prepared for me.[21]

That mission helped Brother Alvarez lay the foundation for his future work. He served as Haedo Branch president, as a stake missionary, as a construction supervisor in Chile, as counselor in the Buenos Aires Stake presidency, as a member of the high council, as a counselor in the Haedo ward bishopric, and as a sealer in the Buenos Aires Temple.

One of the oldest South American members, Antonino Gianfelice stated:

Ever since I was very young I had always had the yearning to serve a mission. I served in two interior cities, Córdoba and Pergamino.

The work of the Church in those days was very slow. It was necessary to be patient and visit the people for a long time in order to gain their friendship and teach them the gospel little by little.

My mission helped me grow spiritually. I found myself engrossed in the work of the Church, preaching to the people, and above all learning that we must always be missionaries.[22]

After his mission, Antonino Gianfelice continued serving and working for the Church. The positions he held included: three times as president of the Liniers Branch, Genealogical Committee, counselor to W. Laird Snelgrove, President of the Argentina Mission, Central District president, Liniers Ward bishop of the Buenos Aires Stake, missionary in the São Paulo Brazil Temple and in the Buenos Aires Temple and Castelar Stake Patriarch.

The Presidency of James L. Barker (1942–44)

James L. Barker

In 1942 there were seventy-four missionaries in the mission serving in twenty-five branches. In August James L. Barker arrived to preside over the Argentina Mission. In October of that year in the Liniers Chapel, a series of branch conferences were held. In April and November 1943, large missionary conferences took place. January 1944 saw the first mission youth conference.

At that time the work was becoming increasingly difficult due to the inception of World War II. As elders were released they were not being replaced.

James L. Barker became known and respected for his devoted work in the mission. During his presidency, many things were organized.

The Second Presidency of W. Ernest Young (1944–49)

Argentina felt the effect of World War II, with political and social agitation reaching the members of the Church. This proved to be the most difficult period for the Argentina Mission since its organization in 1925. According to Hugo N. Salvioli:

> At the time of the war there were only two missionaries, both native of Mexico. I remember their names were Elders Memmott and Call. They were the only ones who remained in the second administration of President Young. They also helped Carl Young, the son of the president.
>
> The elders traveled the mission area and collaborated with members that had been called to preside over the branches. At that time there were no districts. During wartime the Church continued to look ahead to impending challenges, overcoming obstacles, and planting seeds that would someday grow into future leaders.[23]

Memories of That Time

President Young was a very special man. He and his wife visited the members and helped them to realize the significance of the kingdom and comprehend the importance of coexistence. Together with the missionaries they were able to achieve a great deal, even though they were a very small group.

Elders Ballard, Pratt, and Wells preached in this area at Rivadavia 8800 in Buenos Aires. Sister Carmen Escudero, who lived in this house, told me stories of how it was common to see these three brothers riding streetcars and preaching the gospel during their visits to Liniers. Even though I had been born in 1928 and did not live during that time, it was interesting to know that in spite of being so small, we were a very solid group.[24]

Fermín Barjollo

With growth being very slow, the distances between the big cities in the mission made leadership a greater necessity. World War II saw almost a total absence of missionaries. These challenges led to the appearance of the first local leaders of the Church. One of the first leaders was Fermín C. Barjollo from Rosario. Frederick S. Williams described him in these words:

> I know of few men who contributed more to the Argentina Mission than Fermín C. Barjollo. He was known and loved by almost everyone in Rosario and by many others who had met and heard him at the semiannual conferences in Buenos Aires.
> Fermín was a fellow traveler with Elders Christian, Clegg, Jensen, Ashton, and Spencer on the ship that arrived in Buenos Aires on December 22, 1926. He was returning to his homeland after working a number of years in Philadelphia, where he had learned to read, write, and speak English. He enjoyed the company of these young North Americans, but wasn't impressed with their message or their calling as missionaries. He moved to Rosario and worked for the Central Argentina Railroad. He married a young Argentine girl and established his home. His first contact with Mormonism was completely forgotten.
> In June 1937, missionaries tracted his home. He was glad to speak English with them, but really didn't know who they were. Being hospitable by nature, he invited them back. The

The W. Ernest Young family (1935–38).

Fermín C. Barjollo   Samuel Boren

elders couldn't keep their appointment with him, but left an Articles of Faith card in his mail box with the name of one of the elders and a brief handwritten note on the back. Only then did Fermín connect these young missionaries with those he had accompanied from New York to Buenos Aires eleven years previously. They had also given him an Articles of Faith card.

He soon started attending meetings and studying with the missionaries. He was baptized November 13, 1937, at age thirty-nine.

Brother Barjollo was a very faithful member. He attended every meeting and took an active part in the proselytizing work, going with the missionaries to call on members. He also put his knowledge of English to good use and translated lessons, manuals, and entire books from English into Spanish. His first translation appeared in the September 1937 issue of *el Mensajero Deseret*,[25] and very few issues came out thereafter that didn't have one of his translated articles.

He attended every semiannual conference in Buenos Aires while I was mission president and stayed with us at the mission home. He was also a frequent speaker.

During the years when there were no missionaries from the States and the branches were left to their own resources, Brother Barjollo, using his railway pass, spent nearly every weekend visiting congregations in Río Cuartro, Córdoba, and Santa Fe, where he admonished and guided the members and administered the sacrament for them. He rendered outstanding service and was able to keep many of the members faithful to the Church during those difficult times.[26]

Because of World War II there was a lack of missionaries and General Authorities able to give sufficient attention to the mission. It was without a doubt one of the most difficult periods for the Church in Argentina.

In 1948 the activity of the Church increased as the nations of the world were peaceful once again. That year, W.

The German members of the White Branch, Buenos Aires (1938).

Missionaries in front of the Quilmes Branch (1937).

Armin and María Hofmann with their five-month-old daughter Dorotea, Tandil 4626, Buenos Aires (1936).

Ernest Young was able to see growth from two missionaries to one hundred.

Quickly, adversities were transformed into blessings for the Church. It was at that time the first local missionaries were called and the first leaders began to arise.

The Visit of Elder Stephen L. Richards

On February 3, 1948, Stephen L. Richards of the Quorum of the Twelve Apostles arrived in Argentina with his wife Irene to visit the mission. They stayed until February 27.

In a meeting with the missionaries, Elder Richards instructed them on subjects such as "missionaries adapting to the different conditions of the mission with the president of the Church having the right to determine those conditions." He encouraged them to follow the counsel of the authorities.

Elder Richards and President Young visited many of the branches in the mission and neighborhoods of Buenos Aires, as well as the north and south areas of the country. When finishing the visit, President Young commented:

> This is the first time that I have seen one of the General Authorities in the mission in my ten years in three foreign missions. Times have changed with faster and better travel and communications.[27]

Notes

1. In the next nine years, due to Stoof's influence, the South America Mission in Argentina and Brazil took on a German-speaking emphasis. Stoof was undoubtedly a fine man, but his call to lead the Church in Spanish-speaking Argentina was a mistake rooted in prejudice against Latin peoples. J. Vernon Sharp, a Spanish-speaking missionary who accompanied Stoof and his wife to the mission in June 1926, wrote in his journal that Stoof did not seem to have much interest in pushing the work among the Spanish people. After Stoof's arrival many German people were baptized into the church. This perpetuated its German nature in Spanish Argentina. Michael B. Smurthwaite, "Socio-Political Factors Affecting the Growth of the Church Since 1925," Unpublished Master's Thesis, 1968, 10.

2. The elders stayed for a month, and concluded that southern Brazil would be "a splendid field for the future development of missionary work." Flavia García Erbolato, "The Church in Brazil," *Ensign*, February 1975, 24.

3. Frederick S. and Frederick G. Williams, *From Acorn to Oak Tree: A Personal History of the Establishment and First Quarter Century Development of the South American Missions. Fullerton, Calif., 1987*, 70–84.

4. The Brazil Mission was formed and placed under the direction of Rulon S. Howells, with seven deacons, four teachers, four priests, twenty-nine male members with no priesthood, sixty-four female members over twenty-one, and thirty-five children. A total of 143 members and nine missionaries were scattered throughout the mission. Erbolato, "The Church in Brazil," 24.

5. The first Portuguese translation of the Book of Mormon was

84   History of the Mormons in Argentina

printed in 1940. A few missionary tracts had been translated and published a year earlier. The Portuguese translation of the Doctrine and Covenants was published in 1950, with the Pearl of Great Price following in 1952. The Church magazine for Portuguese-speaking members, *A Gaivota* (now *A Liahona*), began publication in 1948. Erbolato, "The Church in Brazil," 24.

   6. With a total height of 2,400 feet, Christ the Redeemer is located in the Tijuca Forest National Park. Construction on the statue began in 1926 at the initiative of the Archdiocese of Rio de Janeiro. Designed by the architect Heitor da Silva Costa and by the sculptor Paul Landowski, it is thirty meters high, spans twenty-eight meters across at the longest point, weighs 1,145 tons, and is built on a base which is eight meters high, where a chapel is located. http://ipanema.com/citytour/corcova.htm.

   7. Two years after President McKay's visit, Henry D. Moyle of the First Presidency prophesied at a missionary meeting in Rio de Janeiro that spiritual experiences would cause converts to enter the Church by the thousands. The Church has experienced such growth—and even with more than forty-five thousand members, four missions, and nine stakes, the work is just beginning. There are literally hundreds of cities in Brazil that have never heard the missionaries. Erbolato, "The Church in Brazil," 24.

   8. Today, Brazil is the home of the largest colony of Japanese outside the Orient, a colony numbering almost a million. Portuguese is the official language, reflecting three hundred years of the dominant culture. Roman Catholic traditions have also deeply influenced Brazilian culture. Erbolato, "The Church in Brazil," 24.

   9. Spanning 1,100,000 square miles, Argentina has a population of approximately thirty million, nine million of whom live in Buenos Aires. The topography of Argentina is varied. To the west are the Andes, to the north the forested plains of the Chaco, to the south the vast Pampas, and in the far south, Patagonia. http://www.travelvantage.com/argen.html.

   10. The Mormon missionaries naturally congregated in big cities with Buenos Aires as headquarters, and the Church grew in this increasing urbanized and industrialized nation. The Church did not send missionaries into the sparsely settled Pampas or plain. A. Theodore Tuttle, former president of all South America Missions, explained that missionaries were sent only to cities large enough to support good working conditions for the missionaries, and which could grow into a self-sustaining unit as large as a Mormon stake. Thus, communication and leadership supervision could be maintained. Smurthwaite, "Socio-Political Factors," 10.

   11. Under the new single-language system in Argentina, the Mormon population grew much more rapidly than in the previous decade. After one year

The Brazil and Argentina Missions 85

Young reported that most missionary contacts were with Spanish-speaking people. The next year the Argentine missionaries baptized more Argentines into the Mormon Church than in any other year in its history, seventy-six converts. The Church of Jesus Christ of Latter-day Saints, Annual Reports, 1936–37, LDS Church Historian's Office, Salt Lake City.

    12. W. Ernest Young, *The Dairy of W. Ernest Young* (Provo, Utah: Brigham Young University Press, 1973), 304.

    13. Hugo N. Salvioli, Oral History, 6–7.

    14. Miguel Angel Avila, Oral History, 1978.

    15. Williams, *From Acorn to Oak Tree,* 10–11.

    16. Ibid., 153–54.

    17. Avila, Oral History.

    18. Frederick S. Williams, "Dedication Prayer on the Liniers Chapel," *El Mensajero Deseret,* May 1939, 7.

    19. Williams and Williams, *From Acorn to Oak Tree,* 185.

    20. Roberto Pedro Antonietti, Oral Interviews, 1978.

    21. José Pedro Alvarez, Manuscript, 1985.

    22. Antonino Gianfelice, Oral History, 1986.

    23. Salvioli, Oral History, 6–7.

    24. Avila, Oral History.

    25. Translated as the *Deseret Messenger*, this periodical was started in 1935 by President Young specifically for the Argentina and Uruguay Missions. Smurthwaite, "Socio-Political Factors," 13.

    26. Williams and Williams, *From Acorn to Oak Tree*, 178–79.

    27. Young, *Diary*, 452.

Chapter 5

A CHURCH OF IMMIGRANTS

Immigrants were usually the most open to new ideas and friendships, and that happened to be a very propitious atmosphere for listening to missionaries. The social pressure was not as strong as that which existed for the native people. The first missionaries in Buenos Aires were afforded much acceptance from the German, Italian, and Spanish immigrants.

The Avila Family

At the end of the nineteenth century and the beginning of the twentieth, thousands of European families immigrated to South America.[1] Because of war, the social and economic conditions impelled them to look to this land as a new opportunity. On May 7, 1910, seventeen-year-old Ramón Avila and his cousin Andrés left their home in Armeria, Spain, for South America.

They arrived in Buenos Aires, Argentina, on June 4, 1910, and were greeted by relatives who had previously traveled to the country. Thus began a new life for Ramón Avila.

Elisa Leonor Melga and Ramón Avila.

The Avila family in 1990.

Dedication to the work and the pursuit of opportunities would dominate his life in the years to come.

In 1925 Ramón married Elisa Leonor Melga, a young Argentine woman whose parents were Italian immigrants. The young couple worked hard and with much effort built a house and their own business. As with many families during that time, the Great Depression of 1930 seriously affected them. However, the difficulties of achieving economic stability did not discourage the Avilas' intentions to establish a large family. They went on to have six boys.

In 1936 their fifth son, José Luis, was born. The year following his birth, he became ill with meningitis. He was admitted to Buenos Aires Children's Hospital for fifteen days; however, his condition only worsened. He was unable to eat or sleep. The doctors informed Ramón and Leonor that they must take José Luis home because they could no longer do anything more to treat him. It would be better if he were at home when he died, rather than in the unfamiliar surroundings of the hospital.

The distressed parents took José Luis back to their home in Ciudadela. There he continued crying and suffering, which only brought more misery and grief to the family. One day their neighbor, María López, found Leonor in a terrible state of weeping. María spoke of two Mormon missionaries who held the priesthood of God and would be able bless the boy. Shortly after they spoke, the missionaries came to their house to bless José Luis. That night he slept very peacefully. On the following day, he started to eat and began his full recovery.

This was a miraculous experience for the Avilas. They approached the Church asking to attend the meetings that were being held near their home in Ciudadela. Sister María López continued to visit them. Since the establishment of the Church in Argentina in 1925, it was customary for the missionaries to work for long periods of time with investigators before baptizing them.

90 History of the Mormons in Argentina

The Avilas were no exception. On October 19, 1940, three years after José Luis's sickness, they were baptized in Liniers.

Ramón Avila in his youth.

On March 1, 1943, a new challenge arrived for the Avilas. Elisa Leonor passed away at the age of thirty-three, leaving her husband Ramón with the six boys, the youngest of whom was barely two years old.

Strong in the faith of the gospel, the Avilas continued on with their life. From his memory, Ramón recalled:

> My misfortune was overwhelming. I had to learn to cook, wash, and iron. I was forced to leave the brick layer office, and post a sign on the front of the house: I fix heaters, stoves, boilers, and clocks.[2]

Both older children (twins), Juan Carlos and Miguel Angel, were fourteen and began work in a butcher shop. At twelve, Francisco worked at a fruit store and the younger children worked at home.

However, the faith of the Avilas never diminished. They constantly rose every Sunday morning at seven and walked ninety minutes from their home in Nueva Pompeya to the branch in Liniers.

Remembering those first years, Brother Miguel Angel Avila commented:

> The majority of the people at that time who attended the Church were hard workers from humble economic conditions, with very few being from higher economic positions. Some owned their own homes, but much effort was required to maintain a family. It was a time of sacrifice, but this was not an obstacle to church participation. We often attended in mended clothes and slippers, and, if it were necessary, wearing our school smocks, because we did not have anything else to wear. We were not ashamed; most Church members lived under the same conditions.[3]

José Luis and Ana María Avila.

The Avila boys stayed in the Church, married, raised children, and were special contributors to the development and growth of the Church in Argentina. Juan Carlos and Miguel Angel Avila were among the first Argentina missionaries, with Juan Carlos being the first mission president called from Argentina. As a small boy, José Luis Avila had been blessed by the missionaries. He served more than ten years as a Buenos Aires Temple worker, and in his last years, was a counselor in the temple presidency. Looking back on the past, he says:

> It was a time of great sacrifice. Thanks to the example of my parents and brothers, today I recognize the blessings I received, meeting my wife, baptizing her, having a family, seeing our children sealed in the temple, and watching our grandsons grow.[4]

The Dömrose Family

The Second World War changed, damaged, and destroyed cities and countries, altering the courses of millions of lives. There were Latter-day Saints living in most of the involved countries who also felt the effects of this terrible experience. The history of the Dömrose family is an example of the clear contrast that exists between knowing and living the gospel of Jesus Christ or drifting in the wickedness of the modern world.

Albert Ludwig Dömrose was born in Klobschin (now Poland), and lived in several places in and around Germany. During World War II he was recruited into the German army.

María Sophia Olling Dömrose was Dutch, and born in the city of Groningen. They married in 1936. They were familiar with The Church of Jesus Christ in that city and after investigat-

The Dömrose family (1950): Standing left: Albert Ludwig, and Maria Sophia with their children Maria Sophia (left), Albert, and Bertha.

ing a long period, were baptized in 1938. Despite the difficult war years that separated the couple, they maintained faith and fidelity to each other and to the Church. When the war ended they met again in Utrecht and continued their work for the Church. It was an extremely hard time. The family was plagued with a lack of work and resources. Europe faced deficits of all types. Overwhelmed by a situation that seemed to never end, people began to immigrate to Argentina. On June 20, 1947, two years after the war had ended, they left Amsterdam headed toward South America.

    The Dömroses had an experience with Cornelius Zappey president of the Netherlands Mission,[5] that greatly influenced their lives in Argentina. President Zappey was visiting Utrecht; and knowing that the Dömrose family was going to immigrate to Argentina, he wanted to meet with them. He blessed them and asked, "Brother Dömrose, what are you going to do when you arrive in Argentina?" He replied, "Look for work so I can suport my family." With greater seriousness President Zappey asked, "What are you going to do about the Church?" "If it's there we will attend with all the other members," replied Brother Dömrose. President Zappey then asked, "But where will you go if there is no Church? What will you do? You need to answer this question."

Brother and Sister Dömrose at the Merlo Buenos Aires Stake (about 1978).

A Church of Immigrants   95

Then Brother Dömrose answered that he had seen himself in a vision of his future. He said:

> We were in Argentina, meeting with our family. We didn't have benches or chairs. There was perhaps a trunk or a table. We used a box as a sacrament table. Neighbors attended and the Church grew to become great.[6]

Shortly after this encounter, with only eighty-five dollars in their pocket, the Dömrose family bought their tickets and headed for Argentina. Albert (47) and María Sophia (37), along with their children, Bertha (9), María Sophia (7), and Albert (1), crossed the great ocean with the fervent desire to begin a new life in South America.

On July 13, 1947, they arrived in Buenos Aires and settled themselves in the town of Ciudadela. In 1948, they moved to Parque San Martín where they struggled to make ends meet. With many needs and few resources, they still continued serving the Church. The new Parque San Martín Ward literally completed

The Parque San Martín Sunday School meeting, including the Dömrose family.

the inspired vision that Brother Dömrose had related to President Zappey some years before.

They met in a modest house without benches or chairs with a box used as a sacrament table. They invited the neighbors and they came. The Church grew and became large. The daughters in the Dömrose family married Latter-day Saint men who went on to serve as stake presidents, bishops, and in other leadership positions. Brother and Sister Dömrose served in many positions, being extraordinary stake missionaries. They returned to Holland in 1966 to complete a regular mission of two years as a missionary couple.

The Parque San Martín Ward located in the Merlo Stake, had thousands baptized in the zone who were descendants from those first Latter-day Saint families.

Even though Brother and Sister Dömrose have passed away, the results of their perseverance and strength have multiplied. Converts and descendants are grateful and continue to love them for their example.

The Welsh Saints of Patagonia

Patagonia evokes desolation, distance, winds, snow, arduous work, and majestic landscapes to Argentineans. It was there, in the middle of the last century, at Puerto Madryn (located at the mouth of the Chubut River), that the legendary Welsh settlers arrived on a boat called the *Mimosa*. They settled the land and integrated into the Argentine nation.

The missionaries of the Church of Jesus Christ of Latter-day Saints who began work in Patagonia in the 1940s found the Welsh settlers with their doors open wide. They were affectionately received and found the people willing to listen to different ideas and types of music, especially religious choral music.

In time, branches in Trelew, Gaiman, Dolavon, Valle 16 de Octubre, and Esquel were established. In 1989 the Trelew

Stake was formed in the Chubut Valley. In July 1990 Trelew was opened up to the provinces in the south of the country.

Today, some descendants of the Welsh settlers are still members of the Church. Iris Myfanwym shared her experiences of past days:

> During the Trelew District Conference I was called to translate the words of Sister Porter who attended with her husband, Elder L. Aldin Porter, presiding over the conference. I situated myself next to her at the pulpit. I felt so moved by her spoken word that I found myself having to apply great control over my emotions lest I be reduced to tears. As I listened, my mind wandered back forty years. I wondered, Is this possible? How can there be so many members of the Church in the Chubut Valley?
>
> When I was young I timidly watched, but listened with much attention to these young people who spoke to my parents. They were Mormon missionaries and they preached the gospel. My parents treated them kindly and patiently listened to their message, but they did not have the slightest interest in the message they shared. Mother simply took advantage of the opportunity to speak to them in English. She treated them like her own children, with respect and love.
>
> One day, one of the missionaries came directly to me and asked, "Do you believe that God created everything?" Clearly I believed in God so I responded to him, "I believe in the Bible." He then asked me, "Even though the Bible has answers, does it ever confuse you?"
>
> We began a serious conversation that ended with the gift of a pamphlet on the history of Joseph Smith. That conversation was followed by many more. It wasn't long before I could honestly say that I knew everything they had taught me was true and I wanted to be baptized. My parents did not give me permission to do so, but they also never denied me the opportunity to attend church. Likewise they never turned away the missionaries who visited. They were always welcome in our

98   History of the Mormons in Argentina

In December 1950, after an exploratory mission to Chile, Robert E. Wells and his companion traversed the Andes Mountains on horseback. In March 1951 Elders Wilden and Waite preached the gospel in Futaleufú, Chile.

home. The missionaries were well received in all the other homes throughout Valle 16 de Octubre and the Chubut Valley, similar to the hospitality they were provided in our home. They were welcomed, treated well, and given meals, but never allowed to speak on religion. In the end, the missionaries were withdrawn and they, along with a few converts, moved to Buenos Aires where the Church was continuing to grow.

As life followed its course, I grew, married, and had children. Still I always held the belief within my heart. Finally I was baptized and my whole life revolved around the activity of the Church. I often thought about how there were so few of the Welsh descendants from the south who were in the Church. I had heard that some branches were being reopened. I found I had the opportunity to be at the Trelew District Conference and was amazed to see an enormous chapel filled with Saints. It was a far cry from when I left that small branch where there were only four missionaries and three investigators.[7]

It is in the history of the Saints in this remote area that the story of Noemí Hughes-Torres, a Welsh descendant, is found:

> The missionaries arrived in the valley looking for my papa. We lived on a small farm about five miles from Rawson. They walked from farm to farm until they located ours. They visited us frequently and began to teach Papa. They rode their bicycles on the dirt road from Trelew. I recall one afternoon they had a Primary class with my brother and me. It soon became late so they stayed for supper. They would frequently make their return trips home at night with lanterns, sometimes in below zero temperatures.
>
> I am thankful for those missionaries who planted the seed for my father. He was not yet baptized, but the books of scripture were in our home. They were always on Papa's table and he used to tell us that it was the true Church and that we would someday unite with it.
>
> As the years passed, the time finally arrived in our lives when we found a great need for the Church and the gospel. There were many copies of *el Mensajero Deseret* at my house and I read about the activities of the young people while Papa read the writings of the prophets. This is part of my testimony. What I read was what I wanted in my life.
>
> On New Year's Eve 1965 we decided to celebrate as if we were members of the Church. We did not drink alcohol and we prepared ourselves to leave on a family trip. I prayed frequently to Heavenly Father that the Church would come to Trelew, and I felt sure that it would happen.
>
> On New Year's Day we left on our trip. Upon returning, Brother Ortiz of Trelew invited us to a meeting with the missionaries who had traveled that way. A few weeks later, two additional missionaries, sent from Buenos Aires by President Strong, arrived with the challenge of baptism.
>
> These missionaries stayed on our farm for a week and helped us with our harvest and daily chores. When the day came, they baptized us in the river that passed by our small

farm. The following week we had our first meeting with Brother Ortiz, Sister Moreira, and two or three other brothers. This began the first small branch in Trelew.[8]

The Church in Córdoba

The growth of the Church in Córdoba in the 1960s led to the division of the Argentina Mission, creating the Argentina North Mission. Branches had formed in most parts of the country extending from the south in Trelew, Chubut to the north in Jujuy.

In Córdoba, the Rio Cuartro Branch was strong for the first time. Later, the work took greater hold in Córdoba, becoming the head of the mission based on the city facilities, the growth in the number of converts, and its location in northern Argentina. Córdoba became one of the strongest branches in the country at that time.

The Pioneers

Juan Aldo Leone, one of the first converts in Córdoba, related the beginning of the work in these words:

El Mensajero Deseret

A Church of Immigrants 101

In 1931 I was two years old when my family moved to Córdoba. My father Juan, mother Líbara, brother Carlos, and I joined the Church in 1940. At the present time, my parents and my brother have already passed away.

In 1938, Swiss immigrant members of the Church, the Bony and Oguey families, had settled in the mountain ranges of Córdoba. President Frederick S. Williams of the Argentina Mission sent two missionaries to the city of Alta Gracia. Because of finding a very adverse atmosphere for the preaching of the gospel, the missionaries remained there just a short time.

Later, the Oguey family settled in Córdoba and the missionaries lived in their house, giving rise to the first branch. It was a 1940s style brick house on the corner. A short time later, the Oguey family moved to Buenos Aires and lived on the corner that was again destined to become the location for Church meetings.

On February 5, 1942, my brother Carlos, Sister Romero, and I were baptized. My parents were baptized two months later. The event was so meaningful that Mission President Frederick S. Williams traveled from Buenos Aires.

I can recall the details of that day with particular feeling. We traveled to the "green belt" area of Guiñazú, north of the city, a land of orchards and farms so I could be baptized in the canal.

For the past twelve years I had wanted to follow "the narrow way." Elder Evan Jones led me into the water and baptized me. With my body submerged in water, my heart forcefully beating, and my feet trying to find the canal bottom, I had finally begun "to fight the good battle." I will never be able to forget the feelings of that moment.

Among the members of that first branch were Laura and Emilio Vergelli, the first converts in Córdoba. I can still remember the furniture in that small branch. It consisted of a few wooden and straw chairs. Two small tables (one for the sacrament and the other serving as a pulpit), a plate glass table, and small glasses for the sacrament were used for many years. The missionaries lived in the branch where they served their two years.

I remember that they came by boat with very heavy luggage and large green metal trunks with golden ironworks that contained clothes for all the seasons of the year. These trunks had a great attraction to the children because of the peculiarities that we sometimes discovered. In those days the missionaries were strangers to us so we viewed a trunk as a true Pandora's box.

Work began on the Church in Córdoba in front of the new Club Atenas on Antonio del Viso. In 1940 we knew most of missionaries already living in the mission home.

The time during World War II was very difficult for the Church and there were very few members in Córdoba. The Oguey and Vergelli families moved to Buenos Aires. When the missionaries returned home they were not replaced. The mission home on Antonio del Viso moved and the members rented a small room with a kitchen and bath on Juan B. Justo to use as a branch. This was the second location of the Church in Córdoba.

Since the missionaries were no longer there, they were replaced by Brother Fermín Barjollo from Rosario. He worked on the railroad and had been transferred to Córdoba. He presided over the branch for several years and was a true spiritual giant. He served as an example of faith and fidelity for both my brother and me. At that time there were no manuals or other training materials, but the classes and preaching sustained us during those long years when meeting attendance was never above ten people. Priesthood meetings were held in the morning with the sacrament meeting being in the afternoon hours. When my family moved to the Alberdi Ward we could not afford to pay for eight roundtrip bus tickets. In the morning my brother and I would cross the river and walk three miles to the meetings, returning home the same way. In the afternoon my family would board the bus for the ride home.

Brother Barjollo maintained a friendly relationship with my parents, which helped us remain faithful to the Church throughout these times. It is for this very reason I owe him great thanks. I consider him one of the heroes of my youth.

The branch on Juan B. Justo continued two years after the end of World War II without gaining any new converts. Later the missionaries returned to Córdoba and a third branch was located on Rodríguez Peña in Córdoba.

I also have memories of Elder H. Clay Gorton (who became president of the Argentina North Mission in 1948) and Apostle Stephen L Richards.

After serving a mission, Ricardo and Carmen Scholz moved to Córdoba. Ricardo was called to preside over the branch and soon a second branch in Cabrera opened. It just so happened that I was called to preside over the Belgrano Branch. The first chapel was constructed in Belgrano and was dedicated by Elder Hugh B. Brown.

Today the Church has bloomed into five stakes with a progressive future. I am happy to know that the dream of those first Swiss pioneers who wrote the mission president in 1938 became a reality. The Lord blessed those thousands of young missionaries who brought the gospel to our land.[9]

Thomas M. Looney, Pioneer of Bahía Blanca

Thomas Murti Looney was born March 20, 1888, in Tocumwal, New South Wales, Australia. His parents, Murti Looney and Agnes Mitchell Looney came from families of Irish immigrants. They had a total of eight sons with Thomas being the youngest.

Later, he traveled most of the world as an agricultural machinery specialist. He moved to Bahía Blanca, Argentina, where he married María Angela Dido who was from Piamonte, Italy. A daughter, Inés, was born in March 1918.

On April 29, 1938, the first missionaries arrived in Bahía Blanca, one of them being Gerald O. Lynn. He had a letter from the Walker family in Quilmes, which contained the name of and directions to their friends in Bahía Blanca, the Looneys.

Thomas, who was always interested in new agricultural techniques, bought a book written by John A. Widtsoe (at that time a member of the Quorum of the Twelve Apostles), and read every word he had written. He wanted to have as much information as possible about the Church when the missionaries arrived. That visit finally occurred on January 18, 1939.

In his diary, Gerald O. Lynn described their visit to the Looney's home:

> March 21, 1939: We went and visited the Looney's and had cake. We left him and Inés a Book of Mormon and *Improvement Era*. Their house is like the lobby of the Grand Hotel with many people coming and going all day long. He certainly is a very pleasant person and I believe that he will be one of first Mormons in Bahía Blanca.

In April 1939 the elders secured the house located at Alvarado 474 to hold their meetings. Thomas was present at the first public meeting held on May 14, 1939.

A few months later Inés Looney developed peritonitis, which almost drove her to the brink of madness. Forty years later in a letter to Inés, Paul Lloyd recounted the following:

> During the first week in November our presence was urgently requested at the hospital because you were seriously ill. Of course we came as fast as possible. When we entered the waiting room the attending physician was telling the secretary that he expected you to die. Soon he informed us that the peritonitis had spread and that you were not expected to live.
>
> When you saw us enter the room, your father (Thomas) was emphatic that we give you a priesthood blessing immedi-

Thomas M. Looney and his wife María A. Dido Looney, Bahía Blanca (1917).

ately. I remember that I felt that I could not bless you with health since there was no hope. I decided to only give a blessing of consolation. Elder Duke anointed you. As I stated previously, I only intended to give a consolation blessing, but after two or three phrases, my mind went completely blank. I stopped speaking, being unable to utter a word. There were some moments of silence and I soon recovered. I recited words that were not my own. Astonished, I listened as I promised you a complete recovery and that God would bless you so that you would live and finish your mission here on earth. While this happened you were completely calm and relaxed. When I finished the blessing I went to your father and told him, "She will be ok." He responded, "It is clear that you know."

Inés Looney Montani, Bahía Blanca (1943).

Never before or after that occasion have I ever felt the spirit so strongly that it completely flooded a room. We were all emotional. When the doctor returned a couple of hours later, he could not believe what he saw. After getting a hold of himself, he said, "By the grace of God she is going to improve." Her father repeated back, "By the grace of God."

Finally Brother Looney was baptized on January 21, 1940. On June 30, 1941, he received the Aaronic Priesthood and on January 30, 1943, was ordained an elder, becoming the first local holder of the Melchizedek Priesthood.

Thomas would accompany the missionaries when contacting investigators and visiting members. Inside his 1929 edition of the Book of Mormon, there are still notes on their talks. Thomas, having a good sense of humor and musical talent, would play hymns on his violin during meetings in the growing branch. He was also able to finish genealogical research about his Australian ancestors and relatives.

Brother Looney passed away on October 14, 1948, before the birth of his first grandson (named Thomas his honor).

Inés and Mario José Montani were baptized on March 31, 1943, by McKay L. Pratt and confirmed by her father.

During the final stage of World War II, the possibility that missionaries would arrive was very slim. The Bahía Blanca Branch had been reduced to a minimum and meetings were held in the Looney home located at Patricios 623, or the home of Mr. Rivera, consulate of Peru, whose daughters had joined the church.[10]

The First Missionaries in Mendoza

In June 1940, four missionaries were sent to Mendoza to initiate work. One of them was Roberto Pedro Antonietti, of Buenos Aires. He had been baptized in October 1936 and was called on his mission by Frederick S. Williams in January 1940. He served his first mission in Quilmes and then in Mendoza. Elder Antonietti related the following:

> When leaving on my mission I sold my only two possessions, a typewriter and a bicycle, to obtain some pants. Sister Rosa Pecollo also contributed to my support.
> At that time there was no training provided to prepare the missionaries. I remember that President Williams entrusted me to be a missionary and he read section four of the Doctrine and Covenants to me before sending me to Quilmes.

Roberto Pedro Antonietti (left) and the Zaldivar family of Mendoza.

My second field of labor was in Mendoza with James Burton as my companion. There we started the work, looking to make friends with the people. We were introduced to Mr. Perkins, a professor of languages at the University of Cuyo, who was also pastor of the Presbyterian Church.

We lived during the month on an allowance until we received instructions to look for and rent a place where we could live and have our meetings.

Brother Burton and I walked for a long while until we saw a place to rent on Aristóbulo del Valle. We entered and asked for information. After leaving, I told him and the other missionaries that we should rent this house. After some discussion we decided to go ahead and rent it.

Nearby we found the first converts in Mendoza, the Zaldivar family, who had five children. They were in the upholstery business and were doing rather well. The father was Vasco (a person from País Vasco, Spain), and a very good person, likable and well educated.

The Cano family lived near the ravine within the city limits. They had a simple house with an open front room where we began to have Church meetings. The mission sent us money and we bought wood benches and a pulpit. The first meetings were very small and frequently only missionaries attended. On occasion members of the Cano family would attend. Soon we began to have a small Primary class.

In first days we tried to befriend the people. We distributed pamphlets and the people were very respectful to us. They would listen at their door, but rarely let us in. My companion Elder Burton made good friends playing basketball at a club.

The first weeks in Mendoza we attended meetings at the Methodist Church and sometimes the Presbyterian or the Anglican Church of Pastor Perkins. They invited us to their meetings and celebrations and treated us very well.[11]

Notes

1. Italians had a long history of migrating to foreign countries as a way of coping with poverty and dislocation. During the nineteenth century, more Italians migrated to South American than to North America. http://www.digitalhistory.uh.edu/historyonline/italian_immigration.cfm.

2. Ramón Avila, Manuscript.

3. Avila, Oral History.

4. José Luis Avila, Commentary, 1986.

5. "Cornelius Zappey had the heavy job of becoming mission president to Holland in February of 1946, just nine months after the end of a shattering world war when the war-scarred Dutch Saints made him do much praying and weeping. They had been occupied for five bitter years by Nazi troops, had seen their dikes that hold back the sea intentionally wrecked, farms destroyed, half the forests destroyed, and forty percent of the livestock destroyed. More than two hundred thousand Dutch people had died. Those who were left were hungry, and bitterness had run deep among them. Dutch Latter-day Saints had not been immune." Maurine Jensen Proctor, "Oh the Rains of Holland, part 3," *Meridian Magazine* (September 2002). http://www.meridianmagazine.com/ prophettour/hague1-3.html.

6. Albert Ludwig and María Sophia Dömrose, Oral Interviews, 1978.

7. Iris Myfanwym Spannaus, Commentary, 1987.
8. Noemí Hughes-Torres, Oral History, 1989.
9. Juan Aldo Leone, "Noticias Locales," *Liahona* March 1998: 7–8.
10. Mario Montani, "Noticias Locales," *Liahona* August 1997: 6–8.
11. Antonietti, Oral History.

Chapter 6

FOUNDATIONS OF LOCAL LEADERSHIP

With the end of World War II in 1945, the Church experienced worldwide replenishment. In 1951 David O. McKay was called as president of the Church.

The Presidency of Harold Brown (1949–52)

On March 22, 1949, President Harold Brown[1] and his wife, Leonor, arrived in Buenos Aires to preside over the direction of the Argentina Mission.

Under his direction the Church began a new stage. While laying the foundation local leaders reaped the rewards from sacrifices and efforts of previous years. Many of the brethren already had experience in callings and lessons on how to live the gospel of Jesus Christ.

President Brown continued the athletic and musical programs that had previously been implemented to gain the confidence of the people. Twenty-five years after the Church in Argentina opened, mission efforts toward German immigrants were redirected to the entire population. In Buenos Aires, Relief Society meetings in German discontinued and from then on meetings for German families were held every two weeks. They printed executive handbooks, organized public sports, and formed radio program committees. Frequently there were articles in the newspapers. Some of them were serious commentaries, and others were critical of the Church. Yet all of these contributed to the goal of making the Church known in the community. According to Hugo Nestor Salvioli:

> President Brown was a spiritual giant who was barely thirty-two when he was called as mission president. Not often do you find such wisdom and force in a man that age, as was the case with him. He had a great impact on local development. He began to gain the confidence of the local members and he granted them positions and responsibilities. With respect to mission history, it is necessary to discuss the Church administrations of those before and after President Brown.[2]
>
> President Brown placed great emphasis on local development and made an obvious separation between the activities of the missionaries and those of the members. He tried to make sure there was not a close bond between the two in their daily lives.
>
> He was preparing the parents and children to attain a prosperous future. By any measure this was not an easy time ....
>
> The Gianfelices, along with Sisters Rosa Pecollo and Lucía Sangirgio, sacrificed much for the promotion of the Church. They were sent from Liniers to Nueva Pompeya to teach. If possible, they would ride a streetcar to their destination, but if not, they simply walked. It was because of them that Primary classes were never without a teacher. The sisters would travel from Floresta to my house in Nueva Pompeya for Primary, making sacrifices to fulfill the calls that they took so seriously.[3]

Juan Carlos Avila

Few men in the history of the Church in Argentina possessed such dedication, commitment, endurance, kindness, and leadership skill as did Juan Carlos Avila. All Argentine Saints respected him.

He served the Lord his entire life; from the time he was young until the time of his death. Although fighting for his health in his last years, he was a faithful attendee at the Buenos Aires Temple.

The Mission Call—On January 31, 1950, Argentina Mission President Harold Brown informed me that I would be the first missionary called for two years after World War II. Additionally, he wanted to call my brother Miguel Angel. Papa explained to him that the family had hoped to finance each mission. This would be impossible if both of us were to leave at the same time. Miguel Angel stayed behind and worked. Thus my family helped me finance my mission.

A Missionary in Rosario—The first area I was assigned was Rosario. Two months later I received a telegram from President Brown, stating, "I have designated you as Arroyito Branch President. Currently the police have the branch closed.

Miguel Angel Avila (left) and Juan Carlos Avila (1978).

Since you are Argentine, I feel certain that you will be able to reopen it."

What the police had done was close the area where the branch operated. They had secured a police strip on the front door, preventing anyone from accessing the house. It was a large house that had belonged to General Lavalle.[4] It had two entry doors, but the police had only closed one so we used the other. In the house we would eat our nightly meals and sleep without being bothered by the local police.

It was a strange situation. I was the president of a branch that had been closed by the police. One day my companion told me that we were going to a secret meeting at the Prieto family house. It was the Sunday for testimony and I was able to meet the members. When I stood up to give my testimony, I began to cry. I told them that the mission president had entrusted me to reopen the branch and I needed their help.

Two Days of Fasting—The time came when we were ready to take down the police strip and reopen the branch. I told my companion, "Let's fast for forty-eight hours." "Forty-eight hours?" "It's possible that we might not be able to do it." I said, "Fine, you do what you can and our Heavenly Father will bless us the same."

Over the next two days we fasted and after fifty hours had passed we were still fasting. Night fell and we prepared our dinner. However, when we tried to eat we could not swallow a bite. Finally we went to sleep without eating.

An Unexpected Transfer—Fifteen days after our fast, a telegram was received from the president. I was to immediately report to Tandil to serve as branch president. I was frustrated and upset.

"It can't be, Elder Brown. Right now we're about to reopen the Arroyito Branch!" And he answered me, "We have prayed and fasted. It is possible that very soon we will receive official permission to reopen the branch."

That is precisely what happened next; almost immediately after my transfer the branch was reopened. I packed my suitcase and my companion accompanied me to the train station. Elder Brown presented me with a box of chocolates and then embraced me. With tears in his eyes, he handed me a letter, asking me to read it after I boarded the train.

The End of the Mission—My father and Miguel Angel waited for me at Retiro Station. We went home and I hugged my brothers, then went on to the mission home. In the release interview, President Brown said he had "fasted and prayed and had been directed to call me as Floresta Branch President."

"No, President. My brother Miguel Angel has to go on his mission now. I have to work and study."

"Elder Avila, you have time for everything."

My father looked at me and smiled.

"Okay, I accept."

A Counselor to the Argentina Mission—President Brown had called Lee Valentine to the position of mission president. At a Church Education System meeting in Floresta President Brown spoke these words, "You have done so much over the past three years that you have been branch president. During this time I have prayed, fasted, and written to President McKay. President McKay has been inspired to call you as first counselor to the Mission Presidency." I was very surprised, replying, "I am not even married. When President Brown called me as Floresta President I had not even had time to look for a wife. Now I feel I must find one."[5]

The Visit of President David O. McKay

Without a doubt, the visit by the Prophet to South America represented a landmark in the history of the Church. Today, through the use of modern technologies such as satellites, videos, and speed of literature distribution, lines of communication between the members of the Church, the Prophet, and other General Authorities are frequent and constant. This circumstance allows Saints all over the world to immediately obtain advice, revelations, and guidance.

Noticias

Nuevos Consejeros en la Misión

El 20 de enero de 1955 el hermano Juan Carlos Avila fué nombrado y apartado como primer consejero en la Misión Argentina, llenando así la vacante que existía desde la partida del élder Glen B. Marble. El nuevo consejero nació en Buenos Aires, hijo de Ramón Avila y Elisa Melga, fallecida. Se bautizó en la Iglesia en 1940, junto con su padre y varios de sus hermanos. Ha sido siempre activo en la Misión, actuando de oficial y maestro en las organizaciones y avanzando en el Sacerdocio. El 31 de enero de 1950 fué ordenado élder por el Pte. Harold Brown y apartado misionero. Sirvió dos años ganando el amor y respeto de cuantos conoció. Pronto después de su relevo en 1952, fué llamado a ocupar el puesto de presidente de la rama de Floresta. Ha seguido en ese llamamiento hasta el momento actual. Capaz y humilde, el Pte. Avila es un digno representante de sus hermanos argentinos en la elevada función que ahora ha sido llamado a desempeñar.

Taken from *El Mensajero Deseret*.

Foundations of Local Leadership 117

To measure the significance of President McKay's visit, it should be remembered that at that time *el Mensajero Deseret* was the only material to which members had access. Of course there were a few Church Education System manuals but those were very limited indeed. It was the mission president, along with the missionaries, who were the main lines of communication for members. The mission president was appointed based on his knowledge of the missionaries, who in large came from the United States where the Church had been established for quite some time.

The visit by the Prophet and other General Authorities was to make certain the members were greatly fortified in faith, knowledge, and unity. It also provided General Authorities with insight that would be needed in order to decide what future directions the Church would need to take.

Today, members who attended so many years ago and heard President McKay, recall with great affection the man and his message. There is no doubt that he touched many hearts. This had been the first time that the Saints in South America had actually seen and heard a Prophet.

The Meeting with Juan D. Perón

Juan Carlos Avila recalls President McKay's report on his visit with Argentina's President:

On February 7, 1954, when Miguel Angel was on his mission, President Juan D. Perón[6] visited the mission. At the conference President McKay told the missionaries that he had met with President Perón. In their meeting President Perón had asked President McKay what he could do for us.

President Valentine made the statement that the chapels were too small for a conference of such great magnitude. Then it was requested that we be allowed to rent a theater for the conference. President Perón offered to let us use the Teatro Nacional Cervantes in Córdoba. It was a very nice facility with theater boxes, but at that time it was being refurbished and painted. President Perón ordered those in charge to hurry and finish the renovations so we could use the facility for our conference. It was clear then that President Perón was indeed a friend to the Mormons. Up until that time there had been some discrimination on the part of the government. For example, they had closed a couple of branches and were not granting visas. It has been said that President Perón spoke to President McKay in English and it was a very cordial meeting.[7]

In his conference speech at the Teatro Nacional Cervantes, President McKay said:

> About ten years ago our son Robert was here as a missionary. I have requested him to interpret this morning. I have to confess that I have certain feelings of pride, fatherly pride, in having him by my side this morning as I bring you a message from my heart.
>
> I have a deep gratitude this morning when I stop and think about the past five days I have been visiting Argentina. I use the word gratitude because it is an external expression of giving thanks. Therefore, gratitude is the same feeling. This morning I am thankful for the opportunity to be here with you in this beautiful theater. I am deeply thankful for the privilege to have met the president of this great republic. By means of his kindness and courtesy, as President Valentine without a doubt has explained to you, we have the privilege to join together here this morning. This president is a great leader and a very friendly host.
>
> I also want to take this opportunity to publicly express the gratitude of the First Presidency of the Church and its favorable attitude toward our supporters and our missionaries who do not take part in the internal policy[8] of any country where the Church is established. By this I mean that I agree sincerely

Foundations of Local Leadership 119

David O. McKay with the members of Buenos Aires.

David O. McKay at the Teatro Nacional Cervantes. Photo by Tato Lencina.

David O. McKay at the Teatro Nacional Cervantes. Photo by Tato Lencina.

with the fundamental principles of this government and want to specifically mention one of them, that is, prosperity cannot be based on borrowed money.

I am thankful for the opportunity to have seen Argentina, this great country that I read so much about when I was young. I even enjoyed the 250-mile trip to Rosario where we met with a group of Saints. I am delighted with the welcomes that have been offered at each one of the locations or branches here. It was a most pleasing surprise to listen to the wonderful choir this morning. My congratulation goes out to them and to you.[9]

Foundations of Local Leadership 121

Notes

1. Reared in the Mormon colonies in northern Mexico, Harold Brown served a mission in and years later served as president of the Argentina Mission. He worked for several years in Uruguay, taught at Brigham Young University, completed doctoral studies at Harvard University, and served prominently in the Church in Cambridge and Washington, D.C. Jay M. Todd, "Harold Brown of Mexico City," *Ensign*, September 1972, 1.

2. Salvioli, Manuscript.

3. M. A. Avila, Oral History.

4. "Juan Lavalle 1797–1841, Argentine general, governor of Buenos Aires Province (1828–29). He served (1816–24) in the War of Independence and (1826–28) in the war with Brazil. Returning to Buenos Aires, he led his troops in revolt (December 1, 1828) against the governor, Manuel Dorrego, who fled. Lavalle was proclaimed governor. He pursued Dorrego, defeated him, and ordered his summary execution (December. 13, 1828). The Argentine provinces protested; a national convention pronounced the execution high treason. Forces commanded by Estanislao López, governor of Santa Fe, and Juan Manuel de Rosas defeated Lavalle (April 1829), who took refuge in Montevideo. Aided by Argentine exiles there and, for a time, by French officials, Lavalle organized an army in 1839 and, invading Argentina, campaigned against Rosas. The campaign was generally unsuccessful; Lavalle was decisively defeated by Manuel Oribe, an ally of Rosas, in 1841. He was killed in Jujuy when attempting to reach Bolivia." *The Columbia Electronic Encyclopedia* Copyright © 2003, Columbia University Press. http://education.yahoo.com/reference/encyclopedia/entry/Lavalle.

5. Juan Carlos Avila, Oral History, 1995.

6. "The military ousted Argentina's constitutional government in 1943. Peron, then an army colonel, was one of the coup's leaders, and he soon became the government's dominant figure as minister of labor. Elections carried him to the presidency in 1946. He aggressively pursued policies aimed at empowering the working class and greatly expanded the number of unionized workers. In 1947 Peron announced the first five year plan based on the growth of industries he nationalized. He helped establish the powerful General Confederation of Labor (CGT). Peron's dynamic wife, Eva Duarte de Peron, known as Evita (1919–52), played a key role in developing support for her husband. Peron won reelection in 1952 but the military sent him into exile in 1955. In the 1950s and 1960s, military and civilian administrations traded power, trying, with limited success, to deal with diminished economic growth and continued social and labor demands. When military governments failed to revive the

122 History of the Mormons in Argentina

economy and suppress escalating terrorism in the late 1960s and early 1970s, the way was open for Peron's return." William E. Berrett, "Church Education System (CES)," *Encyclopedia of Mormonism*, vol. I (New York: Macmillan Publishing Company, 1992), available on *GospeLink* (1998), Disk A.

    7. J. C. Avila, Oral History.

    8. "The religious and political freedoms granted by the U.S. Constitution were essential for the restoration of the gospel and the protection of the Saints during early Church history. They continue to provide important security for the formal "base of operations" of the Church of Jesus Christ of Latter-day Saints. The same range of freedoms is not required, however, to successfully preach the gospel in other lands. Converts join and practice the faith in many countries where the Church does not even enjoy public recognition (much less a tax-exempt status). The missions of the Church work as best they can within each nation's culture and political system as missionaries gather the righteous out of the world into stakes of Zion." Victor R. Ludlow, "More Nations than One: The Gospel in other Lands," *Principles and Practices of the Restored Gospel* (Salt Lake City: Deseret Book Company, 1992), 597.

    9. *El Mensajero Deseret,* March 1954, 6.

Chapter 7

THE GREAT MISSIONS

The 1960s could be called the time of the large missions. A. Theodore Tuttle was assigned as director of the seven South America Missions, establishing his headquarters in Montevideo, Uruguay. This was the time before the creation of stakes when there were large numbers of converts. All areas of the Church were under the supervision of the mission presidencies: education, leadership, calls, discipline, construction, training materials, programs, and plans.

These large missions included vast geographic territory. Buildings were constructed, such as the mission home in Córdoba and Buenos Aires.

The large missions organized the directive goals of the auxiliary organizations and played a fundamental role in the implementation of the programs and the training of local leaders. At this time, auxiliary organizations played an even more outstanding role than the priesthood quorums in the activity of the branches. They worked independently of the presidency of the mission. They continuously supervised district conferences and

President Ronald V. Stone of the North Argentina Mission and his family.

On Sunday, September 16, 1962, the North Argentina Mission was organized. The leaders and their wives, left: Ronald V. Stone, Patricia J. Stone, Marné Tuttle, A. Theodore Tuttle, Edna Snelgrove, and C. Laird Snelgrove.

The Great Missions 125

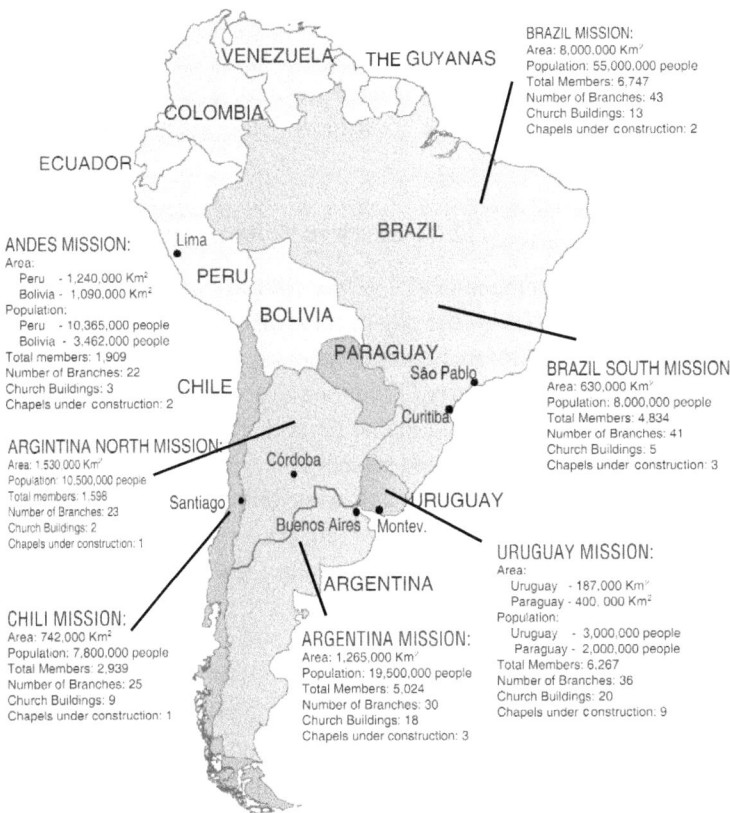

Membership and organizational statistics for December 31, 1962.

included mission commitment in their responsibility to enable and to teach. District conferences generally included one long session of training and instruction on a Saturday afternoon, a social and cultural activity at night, and a priesthood session on Sunday morning.

Choirs, visiting authorities, and leadership were the things all members of the districts desired. The messages of the mission president and his counselors were acknowledged with respect and reverence.

The Church in Salta

On September 15, 1959, the first missionaries arrived in the city of Salta. It was the day of the Celebration of the Miracle,[1] a religious celebration of great meaning in the province, that ended with a parade. Larry Oliver and his companion admired the people of Salta for their faith and perceived a promising future in the spreading of the restored gospel.

In October, the missionaries knocked on the door of Angelica Honoria Yamada-Ariki and spoke with her concerning their mission. Moved by their message, she spoke to her sister Felisa Yamada-Chehda to suggest that she have the missionaries visit. In the weeks that followed, the elders began to teach the Chehda family along with her younger sister Tomie Yamada. In April 1960 the first Church Education System meetings were held in a house rented at Miracle 85. On April 16 the first baptismal service was held. Brian D. Chelius and Clair H. Platt, Jr. baptized the Yamada sisters in the Arenales River. The day was somewhat cold and windy with many storm clouds. They had borrowed a truck and arrived at the river in the rain. They began the baptismal service by singing a hymn and the skies seemed to open themselves as sunrays illuminated the scene. Two weeks later the first men were baptized, future leaders Faiel Chehda,

The Great Missions 127

A special conference in Belgrano, Córdoba. Left: Marné Tuttle, mayor of Córdoba Victor Martínez (second row), A. Theodore Tuttle, Camilla Kimball, Spencer W. Kimball, and Presidents Stone and Fernández.

Open house at the chapel in Maipu, Córdoba. Left to right: Angel Fernández, Victor Martínez, mayor of Córdoba, and Richard G. Scott, president of the Argentina North Mission.

Adrián Chehda, and Praxedes Cebrian. Over the next few months two more Yamada sisters were baptized, Hanako Yamada-Correa and Inocencia Berta Yamada-Ikehara.

They spent the next four decades in a constant persevering faith. With the contribution of many other pioneers, Salta continued to grow. Currently it has two stakes and is the mission headquarters.[2]

The Church in Tucumán

On April 9, 1960, María Rosario-Omill was the first person to be baptized by William Sill. The sacrament meetings were held in the house of Sister Omill. Among the missionaries who were present one memorable was Hugo A. Catrón, who was traveling in the Argentina Mission.

At that time, conversion to the Church led to certain uprooting and life changes. Often converts experience rejection and great social pressure from family members, neighbors, and friends.

The first missionaries in Salta, Brian D. Chelius, left, and Larry Oliver (April 1960).

Nevertheless, at all times there were faithful members who successfully built the base of the ever-increasing Church membership that is seen today. In Tucumán, María Rosario-Omill was one of the first converts to be baptized along with her nephew, Carlos Rinaldo Galmes. She immediately started using his house to hold Church meetings.

Sister Omill recorded:

> When we left the river after we were baptized, Elder Sill said at that time I couldn't possibly understand the importance that had our baptism would have for other investigators. They would see us taking the sacrament and this would be a great help for the beginning of the Church in Tucumán.[3]

After her baptism, the missionaries rented the first meeting house at Honduras 183 and the Church began its slow growth.

The older members of Tucumán recalled converts such as Emilia Farías-Rossini (December 1960), the Conde family (1962), the Craven family (1964), the Sorroza, Lorenti, and Lazarte families, and the two sisters Matilda and Carlota Alicia Mertz.

Emilia Farías-Rossini spoke the names of Paul Mortensen and William Sill with great emotion:

> Their testimonies were the reason I converted. Now I am happy and enjoying the blessings of the gospel.
> The first years of the Church were very special. We were all eager for knowledge. Everything was new. We learned to pray, sing, preach, and love the people. Our life became new, a new way to live and a new way to develop.[4]

Inés Craven remembers:

> In 1961 the first missionaries came to our door. I invited them to return when my father was home. Because we did not

Gordon B. Hinckley of the Quorum of the Twelve at the dedication of the Tucumán Chapel (November 1968).

attend the Church they began teaching us and showing us films.
In 1964 my brother Ricardo became friends with Juan C. Cuevas, who was a member. He invited us to church. My brother was the first one to be baptized. I was baptized soon after and later Papa.

Ricardo Craven was twelve years old when he was baptized. Referring to his life in the Church, he said:

> It was a time of rejoicing and growth. A time in which I was taught the meaning of life, in which I would preach what I knew to be the truth.[5]

The Church in Resistencia

After Reinhold Stoof's visit to Chaco in 1927, there were no other known attempts to initiate proselytizing there until 1960. James Wilson was one of the first missionaries to begin the work in Resistencia:

> First I visited a conference in Tucumán where I met my companion. From there we traveled to Salta and crossed the Chaco by train.
> In October 1960 we arrived at Resistencia and spent the whole day looking for a place to live. We found a place that provided lodging and food. On the following day we began proselytizing and the next day we knocked on the door of an English gentleman. He was very interested in talking to us, but not in listening to the message of the gospel. His name was Copper Coals. He had a small English school and he offered to let us use it for meetings. It was a gift for us, because we could begin holding Sunday School meetings in the first week of proselytizing in Resistencia.
> Sister Lestani was a member of the Church who had been baptized in Rosario years before. She brought her children and we

James Wilson and companion in the Central Plaza of Resistencia.

had fourteen to nineteen people at the first meeting.

Sister Lestani's husband was a recognized doctor who helped us to arrange an appointment with the governor, superintendent, and chief of police. The following week we visited each of them and left a Book of Mormon. We also visited one of the secondary schools and explained who we were and what we were doing. There were announcements in newspapers and everyone welcomed us. Our work of knocking doors was much easier because of the notoriety we had obtained.

Ten years prior, the missionaries had brought basketball equipment to Resistencia, and since then, the people had always liked the Mormons.

In those days Resistencia had a small town atmosphere where everyone knew each other. It was a relatively new, clean, and orderly city with paved streets. Everything was centralized on the main street and people were friendly.

The Church was open to all people but we needed leaders before being able to reach out and help those with few resources. We made an effort to work with those families who could occupy leadership positions in the Church, such as branch presidents, Relief Society presidents, or quorum presidents.

There are fond memories of Resistencia, perhaps due to the help of the Lestani family, and all the very friendly people. The governor and the other leaders showed a sincere interest in the work that we were doing.

The first baptism took place just a short time after my transfer from Resistencia. At that time a person was not baptized until they had studied and investigated at least three months. The first person to be baptized was Sister Barrientos.[6]

Notes

1. From September 6 to 15 of every year, Salta welcomes large numbers of tourists for the Celebration of the Miracle, one of the more important celebrations of faith of the Argentine North. During those days, the town of Salta renews the devotion by its patron Saints, the Miracle of the Lord and the Miracle of the Virgin. http://www.kmxkm.com.ar/paginas/notas/fiesta_del_milagro/fiesta_del_milagro.shtml.

2. Sergio Chehda, "Noticias Locales," *Liahona,* February 1998, 6–7.

3. María Rosario-Omill, Oral History, 1996.

4. Ibid.

5. "Noticias Locales," *Liahona,* May 1997, 7–11.

6. James Wilson, Oral History, 1992; "Noticias Locales," *Liahona,* April 1998, 7–8.

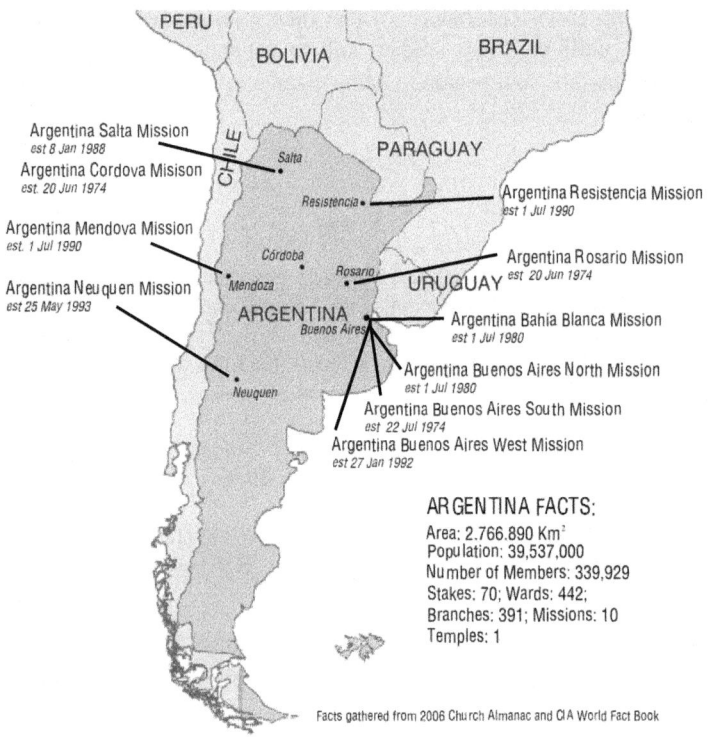

Statistics and Missions in Argentina, 2006

Chapter 8

THE GOSPEL REACHES ALL OF SOUTH AMERICA

During the 1960s, the South America missions expanded. David O. McKay invited each Church member to be a "member missionary." A. Theodore Tuttle of the First Quorum of the Seventy was sent to live in Montevideo, Uruguay, and to direct the seven missions of South America. The program of chapel construction began with the phrase, "one chapel for each branch." The chapels themselves turned into great misionaries since they were the visible strength and growth of the Church in those days.

The Expansion of the Gospel in South America

The Church grew very slowly in Argentina and Brazil, requiring thirty years to take hold firmly. By the end of the fifties and into the early sixties, the gospel had arrived in almost every country of South America.

Argentina (1925): December 25, Melvin J. Ballard offers the prayer dedicating South America for the preaching of the gospel. The South America Mission is established in Buenos Aires.

Brazil (1927): Reinhold Stoof[1] is president of the South America Mission; Brazil initiates proselytizing. German members of the Church have been there since 1923. In 1935 the Brazil Mission becomes a separate mission.

Uruguay (1944): A branch independent of the Argentina Mission is organized in Montevideo. In 1947 the Uruguay Mission with Frederick S. Williams as president is organized.

Paraguay (1948): The first converts are baptized and the first branch is organized. In 1950 the first missionaries arrive from the Uruguay Mission.

Chile (1954): David O. McKay visits Santiago. In 1956 two missionaries from the Argentina Mission comes to Santiago to start proselytizing. First part of the Argentina Mission, it is incorporated in the Andes Mission, in 1959 and in 1961 is organized as the Chile Mission

Peru (1956): The Lima Branch with Frederick S. Williams as president is organized. Missionaries are sent from the Uruguay Mission. In 1959 the Andes Mission, with headquarters in Lima, is organized.

Bolivia (1964): Missionaries from the Andes Mission baptize the first member in Cochabamba. In 1966 the Andes South Mission is organized and soon becomes the Bolivia-La Paz Mission.

Ecuador (1965): The first four missionaries arrive from the Andes Mission. In 1970 the Ecuador Mission is created.

Colombia (1966): North American members conduct Church meetings in Bogota and Cali. Missionaries arrive from the Andes Mission. In 1968 the Colombia-Venezuela Mission is created.

Venezuela (1966): A branch is organized and four missionaries arrive from the Costa Rica Mission.

Guyana-Georgetown (1988): Some meetings are held and in 1989 the Church is recognized.

The Mountain Range Mission

Melvin J. Ballard and Rey L. Pratt arrived in Buenos Aires in 1925. On their return trip they visited La Paz, Bolivia, and Mollendo, Peru, but did not visit Chile, as has been commonly believed.

In 1927 J. Vernon Sharp, returning from his mission in Argentina, informed the First Presidency that Bolivia and Peru were still not prepared for the Church to take root there.

Several Mormon families of the Church lived in Chile. In 1928 Sister Folson and her children, held unofficial meetings and activities as a Primary class, teaching hymns in Spanish to the children of northern Chile.

During their tour of Latin America in 1954, David O. McKay and his companions stayed in the home of William Fotheringham,[2] who had lived in Santiago, Chile, with his family since 1952. On the following day they traveled to Lima, Peru, to visit a small group of Saints.

On June 23, 1956, under the direction of Lee B. Valentine from the Argentina Mission, two missionaries were sent to Santiago to initiate mission work in this region.

Months before, Frederick S. Williams, who had presided over the Uruguay and the Argentina Missions, suggested to the First Presidency integrating the small group in Lima into the mission jurisdiction. The First Presidency recommended that two missionaries be sent to Peru under the jurisdiction of the Uruguay Mission.

Henry D. Moyle, a member of the Quorum of the Twelve, arrived in Santiago, Chile on July 4, 1956, to hasten the work. During his stay he blessed the town with a fervent prayer, prophesying prosperous mission work. He gave the same prophecy in Lima.

Ñuñoa was the first branch of the Church in Santiago. It began with the attendance of thirteen members. On November 25, 1956, the first seven Chilean converts were baptized.

A short time later the Providencia Branch was also organized in Santiago, followed by branches in Concepción, Viña del Mar, and Valparaíso.

In April 1959 Spencer W. Kimball of the Quorum of the Twelve visited Chile and Peru during his tour of the South America missions. A short time later the First Presidency announced the formation of the new Andes Mission, which

The first baptismal service in Santiago.

The Gospel Reaches All of South America 139

Harold B. Lee in the door of the mission home, Virrey del Pino 2130, Buenos Aires (1959).

should inlude Peru. J. Vernon Sharp was designated president of this mission, to which, at a later date, Bolivia was annexed.

On November 1, 1959, Harold B. Lee of the Quorum of the Twelve traveled to Lima to officially organize the Andes Mission. He said on that occasion, "In my opinion, there are no other missions in the world that can count on so many promises as the missions of South America."

In 1959 the Church had chapels in both Peru and Chile. President Lee announced that the mission president would reside in Lima, with a secondary office in Providencia which is located in the center of the Chilean District.

On January 13, 1960, a series of severe seismic movements rocked the south of Chile.[3] Although no Saints were hurt or killed, President Sharp asked the First Presidency for help. More than sixteen tons of first aid supplies arrived in Chile from Salt Lake City. On May 31 of the same year a parliamentary delegation traveled from Chile to Salt Lake City to officially thank the Church.

Robert E. Wells

Richard G. Scott

Hugo N. Salvioli

Samuel Boren

Notes

1. Reinhold Stoof visited Brazil in 1927 and reported that much success could be realized among the German-speaking people of Brazil. David B. Haight, "Planting Gospel Seeds of Spirituality," *Ensign*, January 1973, 74.

2. In 1952 William Fotheringham, an active member of the Church, moved with his family to Santiago. He corresponded with the General Authorities, and in 1953 David O. McKay visited Chile on his tour of South America. Three years later in 1956, Henry D. Moyle also visited Chile; and upon his recommendation, Joseph Bentley and Verle Allred crossed the Andes from Argentina and began proselyting. Soon Brother Fotheringham was presiding over the Ñuñoa Branch—thirteen North American members in Santiago. Steven J. Iverson, "Chile," *Ensign*, February 1977, 44.

3. Other Church reports of earthquakes in Chile include the following: March 28, 1965, Steven J. Iverson, "Chile," *Ensign*, February 1977, 44; July 16, 1971, Gordon Irving, "A Review of the Administration of President Joseph Fielding Smith," *Ensign*, August 1972, 40.

Chapter 9

THE FIRST STAKES

For many years members desired the organization of a Church stake in Argentina. However, the meaning of a stake was not clearly understood by all members.

Leaders were specially trained and prepared by Mission Presidents C. Laird Snelgrove (1960), Arthur H. Strong (1963),[1] and Rex N. Terry (1966).

In order to follow the path of correctly organizing a stake, President Snelgrove structured the Mission Directive Council, following the model of the stake high council. The council consisted of twelve men who held the Melchizedek Priesthood and aided in the administration of the mission. The members of this council were:

Fermín C. Barjollo of Rosario, sixty-two years old with ample leadership experience in the mission.
Hugo N. Salvioli of La Plata, thirty-one years old with twenty-one years in the Church.

Ignacio Lázara of Rosario, thirty years old with eleven in the Church.

Emilio Vergelli of Haedo, twenty-nine years old with twenty years in the Church.

Alfredo Blanc of Pergamino, forty-two years old with five years in the Church.

Antonino Gianfelice[2] of Buenos Aires, forty years old with thirty-two in the Church. He was one of the pioneers of the Church in Argentina.

Horacio Baroni of Quilmes, twenty-nine years old with ten years in the Church. He had served as a missionary and as president of the first quarum of elders in the mission.

Raúl Rovira of Rosario, president of the mission's second quorum of elders.

Esteban Giuliani of Buenos Aires, forty-seven years old with twenty years in the Church.

The Directive Council of the Argentina Mission, 1962.

Robert Olaiz of La Plata, twenty-six years old with ten years in the Church.

José Carlos Franco of Buenos Aires, forty-eight years old with four years in the Church.

Ted Lyon of Salt Lake City, twenty-one years old.

The Mission Directive Council contributed to the development of the first Buenos Aires Stake. It was an excellent way to instruct and train leaders who would someday serve in future stakes.

The Organization of the Buenos Aires Stake

With the same faith, love, and anxiousness that a parent awaits the birth of a child, the Argentina members awaited the organization of their first stake of Zion in Buenos Aires; the wait was fruitful in its preparatory work.

On Sunday, November 20, 1966, under the direction of Spencer W. Kimball and aided by Franklin D. Richards (assistant to the Twelve), the second stake in South America was organized in Buenos Aires.

Also attending were general authorities along with Richard G. Scott, president of the Argentina North Mission. The conference was held in Caseros Chapel with over fourteen hundred people present. Mission President Rex N. Terry directed the first session. Angel Abrea was sustained as stake president, Hugo A. Catrón as first counselor, and Juan Carlos Avila as second counselor. The districts were organized as follows:

Branch	**Location**	**Bishop**
First	Liniers	Antonino Gianfelice
Second	Sarmiento	Emilio Vergelli
Third	Merlo	Osvaldo Borello

The Buenos Aires Stake presidency: left, Hugo A. Catrón (first counselor), Angel Abrea (president), and Juan Carlos Avila (second counselor).

Caseros Chapel, located at the center of the Buenos Aires Stake (1966).

The First Stakes 147

Fourth	Caseros	Juan Carlos Cittadini
Fifth	Vicente López	Egeo A. Gabasa
Sixth	Belgrano	Francisco Herrero
Seventh	Floresta	Miguel Angel Avila

President Abrea directed the second conference session, giving an inspired message and expressing a fervent desire to serve and share his testimony.

In his final speech, Elder Kimball expressed his confidence in the leaders who had been called. He also spoke of Argentina and the beauty of the country, emphasizing the capacity and spiritual receptivity of its people. He specifically emphasized the progress and development that the Buenos Aires Stakes would see over the next years.

Other Stakes

The Buenos Aires Stake served as models to members and leaders located in other areas of the country. In several areas where the Church had grown, preparations were made to organize stakes. The first ten in Argentina were:

Stake	Organization	President
1. Buenos Aires	Nov 20, 1966	Angel Abrea
2. Córdoba	Feb 28, 1972	Arturo Palmieri
3. Mendoza	Mar 1, 1972	Mario A. Rastelli
4. Rosario	May 5, 1974	Hugo R. Gazzoni
5. Buenos Aires West	May 12, 1974	Hugo A. Catrón
6. Buenos Aires East	May 12, 1974	Juan A. Walker
7. Quilmes	May 15, 1975	Hugo N. Salvioli
8. Banfield	May 14, 1978	Heber Omar Díaz
9. Buenos Aires Merlo	Aug 13, 1978	Enrique A. Ibarra
10. Buenos Aires North	Jan 28, 1979	Tomás F. Lindheimer[3]

148   History of the Mormons in Argentina

The Mendoza Stake was organized by Howard W. Hunter, assisted by Mission President H. Clay Gorton.

President Angel Fernández, a counselor in the Presidency of the North Argentina Mission, speaks at the organization of the Córdoba Stake.

Travels to Salt Lake City

Before organizing stakes in South America, some leaders were invited to visit Salt Lake City. There they could appreciate the strength of the Church by seeing the general councils in action and receive instruction in the general conference setting. After the organization of a stake, the presidency, bishops, and patriarch were invited to the next conference. A member of the stake presidency attended each conference thereafter. Being able to interact with the apostles and prophet was a highly motivational experience that had profound effects on the growth of the work.

A first trip to conference usually included visiting the temple, which was another factor leading to increased spiritual growth. Such growth shaped the basic maturity and understanding needed for the creation of future stakes and temple work in Argentina.

It must be remembered that most of these leaders had been members of the Church for years, reading and hearing about Zion in Salt Lake City (the Church headquarters), almost to a worshipful degree.

When they left Utah, they carried back with them a spiritual experience, which on their return, they communicated to other members and leaders. Such testimonies allowed the extension of the vision while specifically increasing the understanding of the role as leaders.

Angel Abrea and his wife, Maria, traveled to Salt Lake City in 1966. María Abrea, who was then president of the mission Relief Society, wrote these comments:

> Within minutes of leaving the Salt Lake City airport, we saw the temple. There it was, like a quiet and gigantic manifestation of faith.

At that moment, everything seemed like a dream. We experienced unforgettable moments, such as the morning of September 20 when we stood in the hall of the Church offices while a door opened showing President David O. McKay coming toward us. We did not dare to walk the few steps that separated us from him; but there was no reason for us not to speak. That was when someone said to him that we were from Argentina. With a kind gesture he invited us to approach so we could shake his hand. His personal secretary then invited us to visit his office. It was a very plain office with memorabilia, books, and photos that marked significant details from a life that had spanned over ninety-three years of dedication to the Lord. Elder Tuttle told us, that in spite of having his office in the same building, he had never seen the Prophet until six months ago at a sealing ceremony.

The ceremonies of eternal marriage and sealing of children were marvelous; you could truly feel the power of the priesthood finalizing the exact idea that when we leave this life our families are eternal.

It was an unforgettable experience participating in general conference. In two of the six sessions, the Samoa Choir sang. They were men and women with a great testimony, who paid their own travel expenses from the Pacific Islands in order to voice their magnificent sound. It always happened that very early in the day people began looking for seats in the Tabernacle, and so it happened during this conference. The inspired messages were generally concerning the family.

It was personally significant for me to attend the annual Relief Society conference, with more than eight thousand women in the Tabernacle. A women's choir of more than 350 voices delighted us with their singing over those two days. I could feel the force of our Church in the world and it only reaffirmed my testimony of the truth. One of the authorities stated that women in the Church should be active in the Relief Society even if they had been called to another auxiliary organization position.

We attended many different sessions in the temples of Saint George, Los Angeles, and Mesa and had similar experiences. There was no greater work or love than the vicarious temple work being performed daily by the men and women during those eight or twelve hours each day in the temples for those who are not on this earth.

Another place transcendent in the history of the Church is Emigration Canyon, the place where Brigham Young first entered the valley, a place that dominates the whole city. What a testimony he must have had to continue forward considering that first view of the valley, knowing there would be many days of work without a single tree to offer them shade.

The Welfare Building is where a great many people with physical handicaps hold paid positions whose duties in turn help others, while at the same time they learn a profession to help them take their place in the perfect organization of the Church.

Additionally, there are numerous other things to mention, the Primary Children's Hospital, the genealogical record vaults, Brigham Young's house, and many more. There are so many memories crowded in my mind. Upon returning home, we felt immense gratitude for our unforgettable experiences and the realization of the Church's conviction that all exists for the benefit of the members.[4]

Worldwide attendance in Salt Lake City for instruction and direction of leaders by the apostles and prophet is mandatory, as stated in Isaiah 2:2–3:

> And it shall come to pass in the last days, that the mountain of the Lord's house shall be established in the top of the mountains, and shall be exalted above the hills; and all nations shall flow unto it. And many people shall go and say, Come ye, and let us go up to the mountain of the Lord, to the house of the God of Jacob; and he will teach us of his ways, and we will

walk in his paths: for out of Zion shall go forth the law, and the word of the Lord from Jerusalem.

The Church has a cultural and spiritual legacy that, over the generations, continues to be shared with members throughout the world. The camaraderie of the Church stretches beyond the national, cultural, and linguistic barriers between Latter-day Saints from all over the world, with Salt Lake City being their common definable identity.

Notes

1. Arthur H. Strong was the supervisor of couples serving as missionaries at Church visitors' centers. He was called to preside over the Santiago Chile Temple, succeeding Eugene F. Olsen, and served as a sealer and ordinance worker in the Salt Lake Temple. His wife, Nedra Heward Strong, served as temple matron. "News of the Church," *Ensign*, July 1985, 77.

2. Argentina's first patriarch Antonino Gianfelice. Judy C. Olsen, "Argentina's Bright and Joyous Day," *Ensign,* February 1998, 36.

3. Tomás F. Lindheimer, a native of Buenos Aires, Argentina, served as director of Temporal Affairs for the Church in Argentina, Uruguay, and Paraguay, presided over the Argentina Córdoba Mission, and served as a bishop and stake president. "News of the Church," *Ensign,* May 1987, 88.

4 María Abrea, Caseros Branch Newspaper, 1:2, 1966.

Chapter 10

THE MISSION PRESIDENTS

Up until the 1960s mission presidents were the most important figures in the Church leadership of Argentina. Their influence at that time was comparable today to that of the General Authorities presiding over an area.

Remembering that Mormonism is a lifestyle, specifically a family lifestyle, converts and leaders regarded the mission president and his family as a model Mormon family. The branch and district presidents, specifically those who were called to work as counselors and members of the directive boards of auxiliary organizations, were given the duties once performed by the mission presidents. The developmental assignments that these men performed and the emergence of local leadership abilities were essential to the establishment of stakes in Argentina.

Presidents including Harold Brown, C. Laird Snelgrove, and Richard G. Scott were examples through their strengths in establishing and training strong local leadership. They were teachers for those leaders.

154 History of the Mormons in Argentina

At that time seminars for branch and district presidents were frequently held at the mission homes. There they learned the basic governing principles of the priesthood.

The Presidents of the Argentina Mission

South America Mission
Melvin J. Ballard (1925)
Reinhold Stoof (1926)

Argentina Mission
(Argentina South and Buenos Aires North)
W. Ernest Young (1935)
Frederick S. Williams (1938)
James L. Barker (1942)
W. Ernest Young (1944)
Harold Brown (1948)
Lee B. Valentine (1952)
Lorin N. Pace (1956)
C. Laird Snelgrove (1960)
Arthur H. Strong (1963)
Rex N. Terry (1966)
Verden E. Bettilyon (1969)
C. Dixon Anderson (1972)
John Arthur Harris (1975)
Joseph L. Bishop, Jr. (1978)
Wendell H. Hall (1981)
Grant C. Fausett (1983)
P. Hap Green (1986)
Gustavo C. Berta (1989)
Anthony Bentley (1992)
David K. Udall (1995)
Craig Hansen (1998)
D. Clive Winn II (2001)
Alan Lee Wilkins (2004)
Shane V. Argyle (2007)

Buenos Aires South Mission
Juan Carlos Avila (1975)
Ireneo Frol (1977)
Lawrence T. Dahl, Jr. (1980)
Wendell H. Hall (1983)
Jorge O. Abad (1984)
Carlos E. Agüero (1987)
Rollin S. Davis (1990)
Keith Crockett (1993)
Stephen Berg Oveson (1996)
Wayne C. Perkins (1999)
Gerardo Vazquez (2001)
Stephen C. Record (2004)

Buenos Aires West Mission
Lloyd H. Richmond (1992)
Garry K. Moore (1994)
Rick Hall (1997)
Rubén S. Tidei (2000)
Jerry R. Villarreal (2002)
Alfonso Ramos (2005)

Argentina North Mission (Córdoba)
Ronald V. Stone (1962)
Richard G. Scott (1965)
H. Clay Gorton (1969)
Marvin E. Brown (1972)
Omar R. Righi (1975)
Hugo R. Gazzoni (1978)
O. James Klein (1981)
Carlos R. Fernández (1984)
Tomás F. Lindheimer (1987)
Gary Lunt (1990)
Craig A. Hill (1993)

Oscar Abrea (1996)
Juan Echegaray (1997)
Enrique Manuel García (2000)
Steven Dale Ogden (2002)
Ron Gardner (2004)

Argentina East Mission (Rosario)
Joseph T. Bentley (1972)
Angel M. Fernández (1975)
Angel Abrea (1978)
David H. Baroni (1981)
Jesse E. Stay (1984)
Guillermo R. Pitarch (1987)
Jorge Ventura (1990)
Thomas Coburn (1990)
Levi Ontiveros (1996)
Rafael Eduardo Pina (1999)
Hyde Merrill (2002)
Richard C. Hutchison (2005)

Bahía Blanca Mission
Allen B. Oliver (1980)
Hugo N. Salvioli (1983)
Agricol Lozano (1986)
Gayle Bluth (1989)
E. Reece Finlinson (1992)
Robert Q. Gardner (1995)
Ramón Alvarez (1995)
Brian Schuck (1997)
R. Lavor Cardon (2000)
Luis Wajchman (2003)
Paul Spitale (2006)

Argentina Salta Mission
Francisco J. Viñas (1988)
Daniel Aguilar (1990)
M. Curtis Jensen (1993)

Carlos Lizardo Pedraja (1996)
David M. Macdonald (1999)
Marvin E. Turley (2002)
Israel Rubalcava (2005)

Resistencia Mission
Wilfredo R. López (1990)
Blair D. Pincock (1993)
Carlos Monroy (1996)
Shirley Dean Christensen (1999)
Rubén B. Luis Spitale (2002)

Mendoza Mission
Charles W. Eastwood (1990)
Tomás F. Lindheimer (1992)
Héctor M. Verdugo (1993)
Gordon K. Thomas (1996)
W. Douglas Steimle (1999)
Cecilio Mario Romero (2002)
Juan Carlos Avila (2005)

Trelew (Neuquén) Mission
Antonio R. Cappi (1990)
Luis C. Coronel (1993)
Héctor Daniel Huerta (1996)
Richard R. George (1999)
George O. Stewart (2002)
Patrick Casaday (2004)
Gary Sorensen (2005)

The counselors to the mission president were carefully selected and called. They had an excellent track record in leadership. Later, many of these men played a fundamental role in the organization of the stakes. Through the teaching they received from the mission presidents, they learned to serve.

The following were the men who served as mission presidents or in other relevant stake positions:

Juan Carlos Avila—counselor to the Argentina Mission, counselor to President Abrea, president of the Argentina Mission, Regional Representative.

Hugo N. Salvioli—worked closely with the Mission Presidents, Buenos Aires: Counselor in the La Plata Stake presidency, La Plata Stake president, Regional Representative, mission president, temple president.

Angel Abrea—worked closely with the mission presidents, counselor to President Strong, Buenos Aires: stake president, Regional Representative, temple president, mission president, and General Authority.

Angel Fernández—counselor to four Córdoba Mission presidents, president of the Córdoba Mission, counselor in the São Paulo Temple presidency, Regional Representative, president of the Buenos Aires Temple and Missionary Training Center.

Hugo A. Catrón—counselor in the Argentina South Mission presidentcy, counselor in the presidency of the Buenos Aires Stake, president of the Buenos Aires West Stake, president of the Spain Seville Mission, Regional Representative, bishop, Area Seventy, and counselor in the first South America South Area Presidency.

The Local Presidents of the Mission

The call of local men to preside over missions was a symbol of leadership and maturity. The time of large missions had passed. The organization of stakes relieved the missions of all member responsibilities and Church programs. With the establishment of the administrative offices of the Presiding Bishopric

The Mission Presidents 159

The Argentina South Mission presidency, President Arthur H. Strong (seated), standing left, Emilio Vergelli (secretary), Hugo A. Catrón (first counselor), and Angel Abrea (second counselor).

in the mid 1970s, the heavy load was lifted from other appointed positions. The missions were therefore able to take care of their primary assignment: preaching the gospel.

In 1974 Juan Carlos Avila was called to preside over the Argentina South Mission. At the end of his mission a great number of brethren had served in that position, many of them in Argentina missions and other South American countries, and European missions.

Argentine Men Who Served as Mission Presidents

Juan Carlos Avila	Argentina Buenos Aires South	1974
Omar R. Righi	Argentina North	1975
Angel M. Fernández	Argentina Rosario	1975
Hugo A. Catrón	Spain Seville	1976
Ireneo Frol	Argentina Buenos Aires South	1978
Pablo L. Gambarotto	Italy Catania	1978
Hugo R. Gazzoni	Argentina Córdoba	1978
Angel Abrea	Argentina Rosario	1978
David H. Baroni	Argentina Rosario	1981
Hugo N. Salvioli	Argentina Bahía Blanca	1983

History of the Mormons in Argentina

Carlos R. Fernández	Argentina Córdoba	1984
Jorge O. Abad	Argentina Buenos Aires South	1984
Guillermo R. Pitarch	Argentina Rosario	1987
Tomás F. Lindheimer	Argentina Córdoba	1987
Carlos E. Agüero	Argentina Buenos Aires South	1987
Gustavo C. Berta	Argentina Buenos Aires North	1989
Enrique A. Ibarra	Peru Lima North	1989
Daniel P. Alvarez	Colombia Barranquilla	1990
Julio E. Chumbita	Colombia Cali	1990
Heber Omar Díaz	Bolivia La Paz	1990
Ricardo Michalek	Chile Viña del Mar	1991
Luis C. Coronel	Argentina Neuquén	1993
Roberto Mazal	Colombia Bogotá	1994
Oscar Abrea	Argentina Córdoba	1996
Jorge Prieto	Spain Canary Islands	1997
Julio C. Alasia	Peru Lima	1997
Fernando D. Ortega	Nicaragua Managua	1998
Daniel A. Moreno	Bolivia Cochabamba	1999

1996: The mission presidents of the South America Area with the Area Presidency in Buenos Aires. Twenty-one presidents lead the missionary force of over four thousand missionaries who work in Argentina, Chile, Paraguay, and Uruguay.

Chapter 11

BEFORE THE TEMPLES

In 1841, Doctrine and Covenants section 124 containing instructions for the construction of the Nauvoo Temple was revealed to the Prophet Joseph Smith. The First Vision, visits from Moroni, and publication of the Book of Mormon all present knowledge of the essential truths in the gospel. The restoration of the priesthood granted the authority to act in the name of God. The organization of the Church was restored, with the first stakes being created in Kirtland, Zion (Missouri), and Nauvoo. As Church members grew in numbers, God sent plans for the construction of temples. Little did members realize at the time, but the first two temples would stretch far past their initial intended usage. The Kirtland Temple would become a preparatory temple for the people and their future endowments while also serving as the house of restoration for essential priesthood keys. Likewise, in the Nauvoo Temple all necessary ordinances would be conducted before the migration of the Church toward the desert.

> But I command you, all ye my Saints, to build a house unto me; and I grant unto you a sufficient time to build a house unto me; and during this time your baptisms shall be acceptable unto me. (D&C 124:31)

> For, for this cause I commanded Moses that he should build a tabernacle, that they should bear it with them in the wilderness, and to build a house in the land of promise, that those ordinances might be revealed which had been hid from before the world was. (D&C 124:38)

> And verily I say unto you, let this house be built unto my name, that I may reveal mine ordinances therein unto my people;
> For I deign to reveal unto my church things which have been kept hid from before the foundation of the world, things that pertain to the dispensation of the fulness of times. (D&C 124:40-41)

Establishing the kingdom of God among the people of the world followed a regular sequence. Missionaries arrived with the Book of Mormon and the knowledge of the truths in the gospel. Those men who were converted were baptized and ordained with the authority of the priesthood. Thus the kingdom was extended. After stakes were formed for refuge, protection, and strength, then came construction of a temple for the blessing of God's children:

> and again, verily I say unto you, I command you again to build a house to my name, even in this place, that you may prove yourselves unto me that ye are faithful in all things whatsoever I command you, that I may bless you, and crown you with honor, immortality, and eternal life. (D&C 124:55)

When the prophet and apostles visited the Saints of South America, they clearly voiced that it was the will of God to establish temples for the spiritual preparation of the people.

In 1956 Apostle Henry D. Moyle told the Saints of Rosario, Argentina:

> Saints in Europe have taken one hundred years in preparing themselves for that temple (Swiss Temple), it was necessary that they have their family tree. I promise that the day will come in which there will be a temple in South America. That day will come as soon as the members are prepared for it.[1]

In 1960 Apostle Ezra Taft Benson urged:

> The Church will continue growing until we have sufficient members to justify the establishment of a stake in Zion and temples in South America.
> This will greatly depend on your own efforts. If you remain loyal and faithful to gospel doctrines, seeking all opportunities to extend the gospel to your neighbors and friends, while at the same time living close to the Lord and supporting his Church, God will use us as instruments in His hands to fulfill His work.

Henry D. Moyle

Ezra Taft Benson

My brothers and sisters, you cannot fail. If you complete your part, the Lord will complete his.[2]

The Temple Ordinances in Spanish

The Mexican Saints were the first to initiate temple work in Spanish. In 1944, The First Presidency authorized translation of the complete ceremony into the Spanish language. This was done under the direction of Antoine R. Ivins of the First Quorum of the Seventy and assisted by Eduardo Balderas[3] from the Church Translation Department. The opportunity to translate temple ordinances was a privilege for these men, who both later testified that the Holy Spirit had guided them.

On November 6, 1945, Spanish-speaking members from the United States and Mexico entered the Arizona Temple to participate for the first time in ordinances in their native language.

This event had been preceded by years of preparation, hope, and faith. On October 23, 1927, President Heber J. Grant prayed at the dedication of the Arizona Temple:

> We beseech thee, oh Lord, that thou wilt stay the hand of the destroyer among the descendants of Lehi and give unto them increasing virility and more abundant health, that they may not perish as a people but that from this time forth they may increase in numbers and in strength and influence, that all the great and glorious promises made concerning the descendants of Lehi may be fulfilled in them; that they may grow in vigor of body and of mind, and above all in love for Thee and thy Son, and increase in diligence and in faithfulness in keeping the commandments which have come to them through the gospel of Jesus Christ, and that many of them may have the privilege of entering this holy house and receiving ordinances for themselves and their departed ancestors.[4]

After checking recommends, family group sheets, preparing clothing, etc., the Saints were led into the chapel of the Arizona Temple where an impressive and unforgettable meeting was held. During three days the ordinances, blessings, and sealings of the temple were administered to the children of Lehi in their own tongue by temple workers who had taken the time to learn the necessary instructions in Spanish.

Spencer W. Kimball also spoke to them, stating they were the beginning of increasing temple activity for the children of Lehi.

> I see the Lamanites coming into this Church in great numbers, instead of coming in small tens or hundreds, they will be in the thousands. I see them organized in wards or stakes made up of Lamanite people. I see them filling the temples and officiating therein.[5]

President McKay acknowledged these Saints in a special meeting in October 1945. On that occasion he told them that they served as examples to members of the Church in Europe, and that all eyes were on them.

The Genealogical Registries

The success of Saints in obtaining a temple is in direct relation to their diligence in preparing family records.

In 1965, the microfilming of genealogical registries began in Argentina under the direction of Sister Raquel Sulé. It was carried out in the general archives.

Later, Emilio Vergelli extended the program of microfilming to include the parish registers of the Catholic Church.

In 1973, Sister Mirta Demarchi-Thompson directed a continuation of the microfilming program. The total registers of the Catholic Church were microfilmed except for a few where the parish priests would not grant permission. In 1978 the program of microfilming in Argentina ended, and Heber Omar Díaz introduced the genealogical program of name extraction to many stakes in Argentina. This program operated under the direction of the priesthood and, as time progressed, it extended to other stakes. Argentina was the sixth country to participate in the program.

The program required thousands of hours voluntarily donated by brothers and sisters. The goal was to extract more than two hundred thousand names by 1984.

In 1980 microfilming completed the several parishes whose records had not been previously authorized.

In 1984, near the Buenos Aires Temple, the Center for Genealogical Services was opened.

On May 4, 1985, the first genealogy library in the Buenos Aires Stake opened. The program was encouraged by the Area Presidency and was replicated in many other stakes in the area.

With the opening of the Buenos Aires Temple and the hard work of missionaries, the task of genealogical investigation and family group sheet preparation was now within reach of the South America South Area stakes.[6]

Notes

1. Henry D. Moyle, Speech in Rosario, Argentina, *Liahona*, August 1963, 184.
2. Ezra Taft Benson, Speech in Argentina, *Liahona*, February 1961, 41.
3. Eduardo Balderas was hired by the Missionary Department on September 1, 1939. Stephen L. Richards, then a member of the Council of the Twelve and later first counselor to David O. McKay, presided over the department, but Brother Balderas's immediate supervisor was the executive secretary of the missionary committee, Gordon B. Hinckley. John E. Carr, "Eduardo Balderas: Translating Faith into Service," *Ensign*, June 1985, 42.

4. Eduardo Balderas, "Northward to Mesa," 30.
5. Ibid., 30–33.
6. Carlos Ferrari, information written by hand, 1985.

Chapter 12

SÃO PAULO, FIRST TEMPLE IN SOUTH AMERICA

Until 1978 it was impossible for most South American members of the Church to attend a temple, because only a few could pay the fare to the United States.

At the 1975 São Paulo and Buenos Aires Area General Conference, Spencer W. Kimball announced the construction of the São Paulo Temple.[1] For several decades the Saints of South America had been waiting for this news.

President Kimball stated that it was a glorious day for South America. He commented that this was the first Area Conference where he announced the construction of the new temple. He then expressed the pleasure that he felt given this opportunity. He hoped that the new temple would be constructed through great sacrifice, because "from sacrifice comes blessings." The one blessing that would surely be prized above the others was the opportunity to be sealed to one's spouse and children for time and eternity. It would be a great comfort to be

Spencer W. Kimball announcing construction of the São Paulo Temple, Buenos Aires Area Conference (1975). A rendering of the temple is displayed from the pulpit.

São Paulo, First Temple in South America 171

assured that, after progressing through this life, families could spend eternity together in rectitude and perfection.

On March 20, 1976, construction began on the temple. Church architect Emil Fetzer[2] designed the temple. He was also credited with the design of the Provo, Tokyo, and Mexico temples. James E. Faust of the First Quorum of the Seventy presided over the groundbreaking. In his message he announced to the thousands of assembled Saints that the greatest challenge would be that of fortifying their faith, a process that began with a great desire to be faithful to God on this earth.

Entire families buckled down and tightened their budgets. Young people willingly gave their entire savings. Those who were affluent donated jewelry and many other valuable items so that they might be included in the sacrificing of the Saints. One missionary wrote to his family telling them to sell the only object of value he had, a microscope. When he received the money from the sale, he donated it all toward the construction of the temple.[3]

For the first time, the words "House of the Lord" and "Holiness to the Lord" were inscribed on a building in South America

A year later, on Wednesday, March 9, 1977, Marion G. Romney, second counselor to the First Presidency, laid the cornerstone stone of the São Paulo Temple. President Kimball presided over the ceremony. James E. Faust stated "With the construction of this temple and the positioning of this cornerstone, we are signifying a new era of the Church in Latin America."

Emil Fetzer commented that the temple could have been constructed without local donations, but that such a decision would have been a grave mistake. When the people sacrifice for the temple, they then feel that it is somehow a part of them and thus showing a deeper commitment. Likewise, President Kimball had previously stated that it was not in the best interest of the people to construct a temple without sacrifice.

The dedication services for the São Paulo Temple were planned for October 30 and November 1–2, 1978. Now the possibility of participating in ordinances was opened to 208,000 members of the Church in South America.

Included in the São Paulo Temple District were Argentina, Bolivia, Brazil, Chile, Colombia, Ecuador, Paraguay, Peru, and Uruguay.

Soon three types of activities began to be performed: eternal marriage carried out by priesthood authority, baptism for the dead, and the endowments, which provided essential knowledge of humankind's eternal journey, which begins before birth on earth, extends through life, and continues after death.

In the interior were rooms for ordinance work, a celestial room, four rooms for sealings, and a baptistery. The temple facilities provided comfort and convenience to aid in conducting different activities carried out in the building.

The baptismal font in the baptistery was made of a single piece of stainless steel with an outside covering of marble. This was the same material in which the twelve oxen were executed. The construction followed the traditional design of the baptismal font in Solomon's Temple with the number of oxen symbolizing the twelve tribes of Israel.

To insure stability, the structure of the building was reinforced to provide greater strength and durability in the event of an earthquake. The outside was covered in plates made of small fragments of marble and white cement, with a final application of synthetic material.

The temple stands 102 feet tall with the golden-colored steel tower rising forty-three feet from the ground, and a bronze foundation in a "V" shape.

São Paulo, First Temple in South America

The São Paulo Temple (1979).

After the dedication of the São Paulo Temple, thousands of Saints in South America were able to travel to Brazil to participate for the first time in temple ordinances. To insure continuing temple attendance, Saints in Argentina, Uruguay, and Paraguay organizated bus trips taking up to seventy-two hours round-trip. The majority of the present-day Church leadership in Argentina received their ordinances in the São Paulo Temple.

Notes

1. São Paulo Temple: announcement, March 1, 1975; groundbreaking, March 20, 1976; dedication, October 30, 1978; rededication, February 22, 2004. http://www.lds.org/temples.

2. The São Paulo Brazil Temple was the first temple built by the Church in South America. One challenge that faced those involved with the construction of this edifice was to find suitable material for the building's exterior in this distant nation. Local stone was not sufficiently white, and the cost of importing stone would be considerable. Emil Fetzer decided to use a cast-stone facing made of marble and quartz crystals set in white concrete. This substance was manufactured in a shop right on the temple site. http://www.familyforever.com/ temples/temples/saopaulo.htm.

3. The South American Saints made great sacrifices for their temple. One widow in northern Argentina donated her home and began living in rented housing. Some coming from Bolivia by bus to see the dedication in 1978 fasted, not only because they chose to, but because they had spent all of their money for transportation. http://www.familyforever.com/temples/temples/saopaulo.htm.

Chapter 13

THE BUENOS AIRES TEMPLE

During general conference on April 2, 1980, President Kimball announced the construction of temples in Santiago, Chile, and Buenos Aires.

On May 30, 1981, at a ceremony attended by more than six thousand people, President Kimball dedicated the land for the Santiago Temple. It was a day of torrential rain, but the Chilean people remained standing for over an hour as they listened to the prophet and General Authorities.

Almost three years later on September 15, 1983, Gordon B. Hinckley visited Chile to dedicate the Santiago Temple.

This was one of the most meaningful events to Church members in Chile, where proselytizing had began in 1954. Now, twenty-nine years later the people were able to witness a temple being dedicated. This was the second temple in operation in South America. In addition to the Chilean members, many Argentineans began attending. Because the Santiago mission already had suitable land for the temple, the dedication had been performed almost two years prior to the dedication in Buenos Aires.

Robert E. Wells was the resident General Authority in Buenos Aires and executive administrator for the four countries in the south area. He was in charge of locating possible sites for the temples of Santiago, Chile, and Buenos Aires.

Hugo A. Catrón[1] was also asked to search for land in the Buenos Aires region. After three years, the First Presidency approved and purchased land on Riccheri Avenue in Ezeiza.

On April 20, 1983, the groundbreaking ceremony for the Buenos Aires Temple occurred. In the presence of forty-three hundred members of the Church, Bruce R. McConkie of the Quorum of the Twelve offered the prayer dedicating the temple site. Charles A. Didier[2] and Angel Abrea assisted Elder McConkie in the dedication. Elder McConkie explained to the people the meaning and importance of the temple, calling it a

> gate to heaven for you and for all saints in Argentina, and for Uruguay and Paraguay. Once the Buenos Aires temple is completed and dedicated, then the saints here will be able to receive every gospel blessing available anywhere on earth. And not only will you be able to receive every blessing on earth, but you will also be able to redeem your dead by performing the ordinances of salvation and exaltation for them.[3]

In his prayer he stated:

> I ask that thou may pour spiritual blessings upon us, and finally when this house pourest spiritual blessings upon us. When this house is built and given unto Thee, wilt thou let Thy Spirit to be here, wilt Thou send Thy Son to visit Thy people here, wilt Thou let the ancient prophets who walked this land and who looked forward to this day, visit this holy house from time to time.[4]

The Buenos Aires Temple 177

The groundbreaking for the Buenos Aires Temple.

The Buenos Aires Temple under construction.

Construction of the Buenos Aires Temple lasted from 1983 through 1986 under the direction of Gary Holland and Argentine architects Ramón Páez[5] and Daniel Bagnati.

The Dedication of the Buenos Aires Temple

Five years after the announcement of the Buenos Aires Temple, the dedication day finally arrived. The delay had only increased the expectations of the Saints. The dedication services held moments of great meaning for families who had dreamed about a temple for the past twenty to thirty years.

Angel Abrea was called as president of the Buenos Aires Temple, with Egeo A. Gabasa[6] and Pablo L. Gambarotto as counselors, and Eduardo Pedersen as registrar. A committee was formed to organize the dedication with Hugo A. Catrón as director and Enrique A. Ibarra and Julio E. Chumbita[7] as assistants.

In December 1985, prior to the dedication, an openhouse was held. Over the course of eight days 29,050 members and nonmembers toured the interior of the Buenos Aires Temple.

On January 17–19, 1986, dedication services took place under the direction of Thomas S. Monson, second counselor to the First Presidency.

The General Authorities present for the dedication were Boyd K. Packer of the Quorum of the Twelve, Robert L. Simpson of the Quorum of the Seventy, the Area Presidency (J. Thomas Fyans, Spencer H. Osborn, and Waldo P. Call),[8] and temple president Angel Abrea.

Buenos Aires North Stake President Tomás F. Lindheimer captured the special feelings experienced by thousands of Saints at the dedication services:

> The temple dedication ceremony spoke of those absent, those who preceded us, and those who have been present in spirit by the grace of God. They are those presidents, mission-

The Buenos Aires Temple 179

Bruce R. McConkie offers the dedication prayer on the temple grounds.

The groundbreaking ceremony.

aries, and brothers, who visited and searched for souls to bring into the fold. We wish these men could have been here. Let us begin with President Benson and his first counselor, President Hinckley, also President Tuttle, who is undergoing an operation (in Salt Lake City).

We lament their absence. We also lament the absence of others such as President W. Ernest Young, who began the work of preaching in the Spanish language along with other brothers and sisters. But the rejoicing spirit of brotherhood is with us whether we are present, absent, or present in spirit.[9]

President Heber Omar Díaz, president of the Buenos Aires Banfield Stake said:

It is a glorious day of joy for all. Members of the Church have waited anxiously for this day, for which many have prepared the way so that we may enjoy this privilege. Now I want to express my feelings of gratitude for the missionaries who shared the gospel with us, who helped the Church journey to arrive at this point in which we can be present in the House of the Lord and participate in its dedication. As it has been said in several of the services, this is a time of rededication-- a time to renew our covenants and to dedicate ourselves to all the holy principles that we have been embracing for many years.[10]

The Dedicatory Prayer

Thomas S. Monson, of the First Presidency offered the dedicatory prayer in the first session and repeated it in the remaining ten:

O God, our Eternal Father, Thou great Elohim. Creator of the heavens, the earth, and all things thereon, we come before Thee this sacred and blessed day with bowed heads, with full hearts and with subdued spirits.

Buenos Aires Temple Presidency (1986). Left: Egeo A. and Claribel Gabasa, Angel and María Victoria Abrea, and Pablo L. and Isabel Gambarotto.

We pray to Thee, our Father, in the name of Thy Beloved Son, Thine Only Begotten in the flesh, our Redeemer and our Savior, Jesus Christ, the Lord. Our thoughts turn to Thee as we contemplate Thy goodness to us, Thy infinite mercies, Thy watchful care and the gift of Thy Beloved Son. We know that through obedience to Thy divine commandments, we may return to Thee and be blessed with life eternal in Thy exalted presence.

We are grateful for this long-awaited time, when Thy house has been completed. The sacrifice of the Saints through the years of patient waiting and constant striving has helped bring to fulfillment this glorious day of dedication. Let peace prevail as we lift our voices in songs of praise and words of prayer for Thy beneficent blessings unto us.

We thank Thee for the restoration of Thy glorious gospel. We marvel at Thy saving doctrines. We rejoice in Thy plan of salvation. Unto Thee we raise our voices in thanksgiving for the lives and ministries of the Prophet Joseph Smith and each succeeding president of Thy Church here upon the earth. Bless with health and wisdom Thy servant, President Ezra Taft Benson, whom Thou hast called to lead Thy Church in this day. Reveal to him Thy mind and will concerning the growth and advancement of Thy work among the children of men. We love and sustain him wholeheartedly. As we pray for President Benson, so we pray for his counselors and all the General Authorities, stake and mission, ward and branch officers and teachers everywhere.

Particularly do we thank Thee, our Father, for the faithful missionaries who have served, and continue now to labor, in this and surrounding lands, who teach Thy truths and who lead Thy children by Thy everlasting light. We remember that it was in this very city of Buenos Aires, on Christmas Day in the year 1925, just sixty years ago, that Elder Melvin J. Ballard, an apostle of the Lord, dedicated all of South America for the preaching of the gospel. What a fulfillment to an inspired prayer is evident today! Stakes of Zion have been organized in

The Buenos Aires Temple   183

General Authorities at the dedication of the Buenos Aires Temple: Left: Angel Abrea, Robert L. Simpson, Boyd K. Packer, Thomas S. Monson, J. Thomas Fyans, Spencer H. Osborn, and Waldo P. Call.

ever-increasing numbers, temples dot the landscape, and faith is exemplified in the daily lives of the members of Thy Church.

Thy sons and daughters have prayed fervently for the completion of this, Thy Holy House. Our tears of gratitude flow freely as we contemplate the precious washings and anointings, the holy endowments and sacred sealings which await the worthy. To know that we shall have the privilege and opportunity to bring to loved ones who have left this mortal life these same blessings so essential to exaltation prompts the silent sobbings we experience.

Bless all, dear Father, who have labored in the erection of this temple, who have contributed their means and efforts to the advancement of Thy work. Bless the faithful tithe payers throughout the world who have made this dream a reality. May each be comforted and blessed.

Now, in the sacred name of Jesus Christ and in the authority of the Holy Priesthood in us vested and under assignment from Thy prophet in this day, we dedicate unto Thee, our Father, and unto Thy Beloved Son, Jesus Christ, this, the Buenos Aires Argentina Temple of the Church of Jesus Christ of Latter-day Saints. We consecrate it for the sacred purposes for which it has been erected. We dedicate it unto Thee as a house of prayer, a house of fasting, a house of faith, a house of learning, a house of glory, a house of order, a house of God. We dedicate the ground on which it stands. We dedicate the shrubs, the flowers and vegetation which add beauty, provide fragrance, bid welcome, and invite holy meditation and inspired thought. We dedicate this sacred structure from the deepest footing to the highest spire. We dedicate each room and hall, every furnishing and fixture, each element and all equipment which have been brought together to form Thy house.

Watch over this magnificent temple. Protect it, we pray, from the storms of nature, the rumblings of the earth, the ravages of time, and from any evil designs of men.

Accept of our offering, hallow it by Thy Holy Spirit and protect it by Thy power. May this temple ever stand as a beacon of righteousness, pointing to all the way of life eternal. As we dedicate this temple, we dedicate our very lives. We desire to lay aside anything petty or sordid and reach to Thee in daily prayer and supplication, that our thoughts may be pure, our hearts and hands clean and our lives in conformity with Thy teachings.

Wilt Thou, our Father, continue to bless the seed of Abraham, Isaac, and Jacob and likewise the descendants of Lehi and Nephi, that the promises contained in the Holy Bible and in the Book of Mormon may be brought to fulfillment and our homes and families blessed abundantly.

May all who enter this, Thy house, be privileged to say, as did the Psalmist of old, "We took sweet counsel together, and walked unto the house of God in company."

We express to Thee our abiding love. We desire to honor Thee and Thy Son each day of our lives. May our posterity fol-

Buenos Aires Temple (1996).

low the example of Thy Son and "increase in wisdom and stature, and in favour with God and man" [Luke 2:52]. We pray Thou wilt accept of our offering and hallow this house which we have built. Bless our lives. Magnify our service and prosper Thy work.

May we, Thy children, be pure and holy before Thee, thereby meriting Thy bounteous blessings and Thy watchful care, we pray in the name of Thy Beloved Son, even the name of Jesus Christ, the Lord. Amen.[11]

Notes

1. In 1976, Hugo A. Catrón was one of the forty-one new mission presidents called by the First Presidency, eight of whom served in newly created missions. He was assigned from the Spanish-speaking mission of Buenos Aires to the Spain Seville. "News of the Church," *Ensign*, June 1976, 86.

2. Charles A. Didier became the Church's Executive Administrator for Europe, presiding over fourteen missions. Later, he would be assigned to supervise the Church's activities in Canada, then, in 1981 to supervise the missions and stakes in Argentina, Paraguay, and Uruguay. With the calling of thirteen new Area Presidencies in 1984, he assumed duties as president of the South America North Area which originally included Brazil, but is now comprised of Ecuador, Venezuela, Colombia, Peru, Bolivia, Surinam, Guyana, and French Guyana. Elder Didier resides in Quito, capital of Ecuador. Edwin O. Haroldsen, "Elder Charles Didier," *Tambuli*, September 1988, 17.

3. Bruce R. McConkie, "Groundbreaking for 4th temple in South America," *Church News*, 1 May 1983, 4

4. Bruce R. McConkie, prayer of dedication on the Buenos Aires Temple land, *Liahona*, Local News, October 1984, 4.

5. Ramón B. Páez, second counselor in the bishopric of the Centro Ward, Mar del Plata Argentina Stake. He recalls that when he was chosen to be the Argentine architect on the temple project, he was admonished to remember that he was working for a "very special client"—the Lord. "News of the Church," *Ensign*, January 1986, 80.

6. In 1987, Egeo Angel Gabasa, of Buenos Aires, Argentina, presided

over the Buenos Aires Temple with his wife, Claribel, as the new temple matron. He had earlier served as a recorder at the Los Angeles Temple, as a bishop, and as a patriarch. "News of the Church," *Ensign*, October 1987, 80.

7. The coming of the temple has had its effect on the lives of many members, including youth. Julio E. Chumbita, director of the LDS Institute of Religion in downtown Buenos Aires, which serves students of several schools, recalls walking among the tents one night on a Church camp-out when he was unable to sleep. He could not avoid hearing what three young men were talking about in their tent; they were earnestly discussing the qualities they hoped to find in their future wives and their desire to be sealed to them in the temple. "News of the Church," *Ensign*, January 1986, 80.

8. Elder Waldo Pratt Call was born in Colonia Juárez, Mexico, but was raised in Colonia Dublan. He was the third of thirteen children. "In our home," he said, "English was usually spoken, although some words or expressions were more easily said in Spanish." Janet Peterson, "Friend to Friend," *Friend* (April 1987): 6.

9. *Liahona,* November 1989, 11

10. Ibid.

11. *Liahona,* April 1986, 3-4.

Chapter 14

THE AREA PRESIDENCIES

In March 1835, God revealed the crucial elements of Church government to Joseph Smith. Doctrine and Covenants 107 states the functions and responsibilities of the quorum presidents, the First Presidency, the Quorum of the Twelve, and the Quorum of the Seventy. These organizations, "upheld by the confidence, faith, and prayer of the church, form a quorum of the Presidency of the Church." (D&C 107:22)

> And they form a quorum, equal in authority to that of the Twelve special witnesses or Apostles just named. (D&C 107:26)

This section then describes the functions of these Church general quorums:

> The Twelve are a Traveling Presiding High Council, to officiate in the name of the Lord, under the direction of the Presidency of the Church, agreeable to the institution of

heaven; to build up the church, and regulate all the affairs of the same in all nations.

The Seventy are to act in the name of the Lord, under the direction of the Twelve or the traveling high council, in building up the church and regulating all the affairs of the same in all nations. (D&C 107:33–34).

This is the governmental organization of The Church of Jesus Christ of Latter-day Saints. With the Church membership's huge growth during the second half of the twentieth century, there was a need for reconstituting the Quorums of the Seventy, and they functioned with the same direction the Lord had given them from the beginning of the Church.

In 1985 the institution of Area Presidencies had a great significance for the commencement and fortification of the Church throughout the world.

Nineteen eighty-four was a landmark year in the South America South Area. In the future, those who write the history of the Church will remember this era as one of the most significant in Church government. It was during July that the majority of Church work all over the world was decentralized by installing Area Presidencies.

At that time the Church was established in ninety-six nations and in eighteen colonies, territories, or possessions. Thirteen Area Presidencies directed these missions, stakes, districts, wards, and branches. Each Area Presidency was composed of three General Authorities who were members of the Quorum of the Seventy. These brethren would serve in their position on a rotating basis.

The international areas were Europe (British Isles, Europe, Africa) with its headquarters in Frankfurt, Germany; Pacific (Australia, New Zealand, Pacific Islands, Hawaii) with its headquarters in Sidney, Australia; Asia (Japan, Korea, Hong

Kong, Taiwan, Southeast Asia, Philippines) with its headquarters in Tokyo, Japan; Mexico-Central America (Mexico, Guatemala, Honduras, Costa Rica, Panama, El Salvador, Nicaragua) with its headquarters in Mexico City, Mexico; South America North (Brazil, Venezuela, Colombia, Ecuador, Peru, Bolivia) with its headquarters in São Paulo, Brazil; and South America South (Argentina, Uruguay, Paraguay, Chile) with its headquarters in Buenos Aires, Argentina.

The First Presidency had initially announced the concept of Area Presidencies in the summer of 1984. However, as a test, only three presidencies were sent to their international areas to reside. The South America South Area, with its seat in Buenos Aires, Argentina, was one of the first three areas announced for this pilot program.

The Presidency of the South America South Area

On June 24, 1984, when the First Presidency announced the concept of area administration for the Church, three veterans with ample Church service experience were carefully selected to direct the South America South Area. A. Theodore Tuttle, a Church educator who was called to the First Quorum of the Seventy in 1958, was named area president. Then serving as Provo Temple president, he would return to South America where he had been a director of the South America Mission headquartered was in Montevideo, Uruguay in the 1960s.

First counselor in the Area Presidency, Jacob de Jager, had been a member of the First Quorum of the Seventy since 1976. A native of Holland and employed by an international electronics company, he had lived in many parts of the world, including Mexico. Elder de Jager served in many positions of Church responsibility, including regional representative.

A. Theodore Tuttle

J. Thomas Fyans

Waldo P. Call

Jacob de Jager

The Area Presidencies 193

Lynn A. Mickelsen

John B. Dickson

Carlos H. Amado

Spencer H. Osborn, a clothing manufacturer in Salt Lake City, had been a fulltime regional representative in the Philippines, mission president, counselor in the Salt Lake City Temple presidency, and stake president with extensive welfare responsibilities. He was called to the First Quorum of the Seventy in April 1984 and was one of the first General Authorities to be called for three to five years.

Instituting Area Presidencies

On August 12–13, 1984, special meetings were held in the Buenos Aires Church offices. A delegation of General Authorities presented the new Area Presidency position to Church leaders and employees. Elder Boyd K. Packer of the Quorum of the Twelve declared "This is an historic moment. The Lord has decided it is time to make some organizational changes in Church government." He explained that, due to the growth in the number of members, the world had been divided into thirteen areas, each one presided over by an Area Presidency.

Elder Packer stated, "Danger comes with growth, as illustrated in the Book of Mormon. This is why we organized ourselves, to avoid that danger. The Church knows the correct way. The revelation channels are open."

Elder Packer indicated that, in the organization of the Church, instruction would come whenever God deemed it necessary.

During the presentation, Elder Packer emphasized his association with Elder Tuttle that had begun forty years prior. "He is a teacher, a man without deception, but with a weakness. He works too much." Elder Packer requested support for President Tuttle to help ease his workload.

Elder Packer declared in a special testimony that angels have not stopped visiting the earth to help with the direction of the Church. "We should have a spirit of cooperation and I promise we will see great things."[1]

Elder Bruce R. McConkie, also of the Quorum of the Twelve and long associated with the Church in South America, emphasized that when Brigham Young died in 1877, the Church had 200,000 members and thirty-four stakes, but that Argentina, Uruguay, Paraguay, and Chile alone had 300,000 members, sev-

Area Presidency (1986). Left: Waldo P. Call, second counselor, J. Thomas Fyans, president, and Ted E. Brewerton, first counselor.

Area Presidency (1994). Left: Horacio A. Tenorio, first counselor, Lynn A. Mickelsen, president, and John B. Dickson, second counselor.

Area Presidency (1997). Left: Carlos H. Amado, first counselor, John B. Dickson, president, and Hugo A. Catrón, second counselor.

enty-seven stakes, a temple in Chile, and another one under construction in Argentina. Elder McConkie stated that this growth was why it was necessary to organize Area Presidencies. He then presented an organizational chart. In Buenos Aires, Joseph C. Muren would report to the Area Presidency, and in Santiago, Jeffrey T. Allred was chosen. Elder McConkie expressed, "This organizational method will emphasize the spiritual nature of the kingdom, allow us to govern ourselves in a new way, and prepare the people for the second coming of Christ."[2]

J. Richard Clarke, of the presiding bishopric, stated, "What we do here today is destined to provide more unity to all members of the Church. The presiding bishopric agrees completely and supports this revelation."[3]

President Tuttle then instructed the new Area Presidency on its course of action: He expressed:

> Emphasis must be placed on scriptures, revelations, ordinances, and doctrines. We have a temple under construction in Argentina and one operating in Chile. It is our duty to prepare each member for the temple, in order that they may receive their endowments. If we unite, we will achieve this goal. I want to emphasize to you the challenge to learn the gospel, live it better, share it, and to redeem our dead.[4]

Elder Jacob de Jager bore a testimony that encouraged dedication and service: "As leaders, we should be worthy Saints, examples to others, carry a temple recommend, and not say go to the temple but say come to the temple with me and do the things that I am doing."[5]

Meetings similar to those in Buenos Aires were held in the Santiago Temple and received with the same enthusiasm as that displayed in Buenos Aires.

Notes

1. Boyd K. Packer, Special meetings, Buenos Aires Church offices, August 12–13, 1984.
2. Bruce R. McConkie, Special meetings, Buenos Aires Church offices, August 12–13, 1984.
3. J. Richard Clarke, Special meetings, Buenos Aires Church offices, August 12–13, 1984.
4. A. Theodore Tuttle, Special meetings, Buenos Aires Church offices, August 12–13, 1984.
5. Jacob de Jager, Special meetings, Buenos Aires Church offices, August 12–13, 1984.

Chapter 15

THE CHALLENGE OF SELF-SUFFICIENCY

In 1974, President Spencer W. Kimball announced to the Regional Representatives of the Church concerning his vision of growth in the kingdom:

> Our responsibility is clear, to preach the gospel everywhere, without exception.
> The Lord is prepared to open all doors, even politically, by breaking the resistance of the nations so that they too may receive the missionaries.
> That is, dear brothers, the belief in which I wanted to share with you today. In preparation for our entry, we must begin with the development of a great mission, a great force in number, and enhanced preparation for the assignment that we must undertake.
> We have local representatives who are fluent in the language and confident in their interactions, knowing when they fulfill their missions, they will be called as bishops, stake pres-

idents, and members of the stake high council to spread the gospel in their land.[1]

Two areas can be identified where the Church in Argentina has grown but still requires greater effort: the development of leadership and the establishment of a resilient mission force.

The success of self-sufficiency relies strongly upon the leadership that contributes to the fortification and expansion of the Church. Two primary characteristics of this leadership occur when a person possesses the capacity (which increases through the direction of the apostles and prophet) to be guided by the Spirit and then develops directional abilities based solely on the gospel principles.

By the work of the leaders who possessed such qualities, the growth of the Church has been possible. In the beginning of the Church's growth in Argentna, Melvin J. Ballard, mission presidents, and missionaries were very important. Among those presidents appointed by the Church, the most outstanding are remembered: Frederick S. Williams in the '40s, Harold Brown in the '50s, A. Theodore Tuttle in the '60s, Robert E. Wells in the '70s and '80s, and after those leaders, the Area Presidencies. These men exerted a strong formative influence on local leadership.

Among the first local leaders was Fermín C. Barjollo of Rosario who had served in North Argentina since World War II.

Later, the brethren in Buenos Aires that stood out were Samuel Boren,[2] Juan Carlos Avila, Antonino Gianfelice, and Angel Abrea. There was also Angel Fernández in Córdoba, Hugo N. Salvioli in La Plata, and Hugo R. Gazzoni of San Nicolás and Rosario.

The Challenge of Self-Sufficiency 201

Elder Angel Abrea

Elder Abrea grew up in a family with strong moral principles. His mother, Zulema Estrada-Abrea,[3] was a member of the Church. She helped him understand the stories contained in the Book of Mormon. In November 1943, at the age of ten, she also assisted him in making the decision to be baptized. He progressed rapidly during his adolescent years, enduring and overcoming great hardships. At barely eighteen years of age, he served as counselor in the district presidency. By twenty-three he was a branch president and later district president. He then went on to serve as stake president, regional representative, and mission president before being sustained on April 4, 1981, as a member of the First Quorum of the Seventy.

He also served as administrative director for the Church Temple Department. After he was called as the first Buenos Aires Temple president, he was the executive administrator of the Bolivia-Peru Mission, and counselor to the Area Presidency of the Mexico-Central America Mission.

He worked diligently with his father who instructed him in the basic principles of commerce, thus resulting in his study of accounting. He taught accounting classes, in one of whom he met María Victoria Chiapparino, whom he married in 1957. After nine years, they were sealed in the Salt Lake City Temple.

From the time she married him, they led a life of service to the Lord. Sister Abrea became president of the mission Relief Society at a very young age. She was also a dedicated seminary teacher who served with great enthusiasm.

Sister Abrea commented that the Church was firmly established in Argentina and has had great influence during the past several decades. Her nieces and nephews represent fourth-generation Church members on her husband's side; and her grandson James Patrick Houlin,[4] born June 6, 1985, is the fourth generation of her family.

Elder Abrea feels that the hand of God is on the nations of South America and that the Church on this earth must surpass the challenges that the ever-increasing number of members brings.

"I am a witness of the latter-day miracles," Elder Abrea affirms. He continued:

> We need to look at what the Church is doing with the eyes of faith. There are so many miracles being done in South America. Members who look beyond the routine affairs of the organization will see the hand of God at work.[5]

Concerning the leadership in South America, it can be said without a doubt that Angel Abrea is one of the greatest leaders known.

"One of the Strongest in the Kingdom"

The apostles and prophet declared that further analysis was required in order to determine the future role of the Church in South America.[6]

When Melvin J. Ballard arrived in Buenos Aires in 1925, the Church had approximately half a million members. This was the direct result of missionary efforts and internal growth over the past ninety-five years (1830–1925). Preaching in the nineteenth century included an invitation to gather to Zion in the Rocky Mountains. Thousands of Europeans crossed the Atlantic on their way to Salt Lake City, establishing a firm base for the Church.

In 1947, more than a century after its organization, the Church reached one million members, with the majority of the members being concentrated in Utah and Idaho. Only sixteen

The Challenge of Self-Sufficiency 203

Gabriel Saez of the Belgrano, Buenos Aires Stake. He was sent as a missionary to the Ukraine in 1994. He represents a growing number of Argentine missionaries that are being sent to other countries.

The Area Presidency with the Area Seventy Authorities. Left: David López, Carlos E. Agüero, Antonio R. Cappi, Carlos H. Amado, John B. Dickson, Hugo A. Catrón, Jorge Ventura, Claudio Zivic, and Jorge L. del Castillo.

years later in 1963 it reached two million. Eight years later in 1971, Church membership had grown to three million. By 1998 it had reached ten million members. Thus, in sixteen years between 1971 and 1998, the Church had experienced a growth of approximately seven million members.

South America was one of the areas of the world that experienced greater growth. In seventy years (1925–1995), two hundred thousand grew to two million.

On July 4, 1926, in his farewell, Melvin J. Ballard made a prophetic declaration to the Saints in Buenos Aires. This declaration said, "The South America Mission would be strong in the kingdom" and would be "a power in the Church."

It is important to understand the significance of being "strong in the kingdom" and "a power." This declaration by Elder Ballard gave the South American members a feeling of happiness and renewed dedication.

To be strong and powerful in the kingdom means to respond to the callings of the prophets, to sacrifice, to consecrate or devote oneself, to complete assignments, to be worthy, to be faithful, diligent, and conscious of spiritual and the temporal responsibilities. This strength and power became visible by the number of converts that the missionaries had baptized through their direction and service, in the work at the temples, and by the consecration of tithes and offerings.

The growth of the Church all over the world continues to prove the spiritual strength and dignity of its individual members.

The pioneers who laid the foundations of the Church in the nineteenth century demonstrated extraordinary heroic effort. The members of today face different challenges in a complex world that generally opposes the values of the gospel. Present challenges require the development of a character similar to that of the pioneers.

The Challenge of Self-Sufficiency 205

How did South America become a strengthening power in the Church? There are some factors that can be identified. There are, prophets, and apostles who have declared these inspired matters. Looking back, growth and strength can be seen in the following areas:

Increasing Number of Young Missionaries—This point is particularly important, not only for the proselytizing work that the missionaries provide, but also in the preparation they receive for their future lives of creating families and leading in the Church.

Temple Work—In this there are signs of strength not by just attending the temple regularly, but also by family history research to do the temple work of ancestors.

Leadership Preparation—This is one of the central strengthening aspects of the Church. The large number of returning missionaries, many being third generation in the Church, assure ample leadership in the future.

Personal and Family Preparation—At one time the members of the Church in Argentina were mainly from low socioeconomic levels. This was not a limitation as far as their faith and consecration were concerned, but concern was voiced as to their development of leadership abilities and economic security.

It was very common in the 1960s and 1970s that young people took such an active interest in their Church obligations, that they postponed or neglected their education.

At the present time a greater balance is observed. More young people are pursuing higher education and many members of the Church have well-paying jobs.

These and other factors will continue to contribute substantially to the growth and strength of the Church in Argentina and South America over the next decades, thus fulfilling Melvin

J. Ballard's words, "a power in the Church, one of the strongest in the kingdom."

Notes

1. Words of President Spencer W. Kimball, transcribed from the film *Go to All the World*.

2. Born in Argentina to a Protestant father and a Catholic mother, Samuel Boren did not soon follow his father into Mormonism. He experienced familiarity with the Church and still remained uncommitted. Baptized on September 12, 1936, he became an active Mormon with many firsts to his credit: first native Argentine to serve a fulltime mission in Argentina, in the first group of members to be chosen to preside over a branch of the Church, first Argentine member to serve in a mission presidency, called by the First Presidency to serve on the first Church building committee in South America in 1961 during which time he also served in the mission presidencies of Uruguay and Argentina. He married an Argentine member of Dutch and Austrian stock, Clara Lorenzi, and with their three chidren immigrated to the United States in 1952. They returned so Brother Boren could serve as head accountant in the Peronista government in 1955, even though he admitted to them that he was not a Peronista. W. Ernest Young rates him as a natural leader and one of the outstanding baptisms of his "first" mission. Personal interview by Michael B. Smurthwaite with Samuel Boren July 14, 1967, Mesa, Arizona.

3. Angel Abrea represents the major European influences in Argentina's heritage. One of his grandfathers was from Italy, the other from Spain. Both of his grandmothers were Argentine-born. His father, Edealo Abrea, was a middle-class businessman. Edealo and Zulema Estrada-Abrea, were fine people who provided moral and ethical examples for their two children, Angel and his younger brother, Oscar. Not active in the dominant religion of Argentina, the family seemed to be waiting, Elder Abrea recalls, "for something to believe in, and that was the message of the Latter-day Saints' Church." It would be satisfying to write that Edealo Abrea joined his wife and sons in Church membership before his death, but that did not happen. Elder Abrea's father nevertheless supported his family, encouraging his wife and sons in their Church service. Searle, "Elder Angel Abrea," *Liahona*, December 1985, 23.

4. James Patrick is the son of their daughter Patricia and her husband Guillermo Houlin. Searle, Ibid., 23.

5. Ibid., 23–26.
6. Ballard, M. Russell, "The Kingdom Rolls Forth in South America," *Ensign,* May 1986, 12

Chapter 16

A NEW CENTURY

The future of the Church has been described by past prophets. The preface of the Doctrine and Covenants is one example of this. On November 1, 1831, in Hiram, Ohio, the Lord said to the Prophet Joseph Smith:

> Hearken ye people from afar; and ye that are upon the islands of the sea, listen together.
> For verily the voice of the Lord is unto all men, and there is none to escape; and there is no eye that shall not see, neither ear that shall not hear, neither heart that shall not be penetrated.
> And the rebellious shall be pierced with much sorrow; for their iniquities shall be spoken upon the housetops, and their secret acts shall be revealed.
> And the voice of warning shall be unto all people, by the mouths of my disciples, whom I have chosen in these last days. (D&C 1:1–4)

To fully understand the true prophetic character of this revelation, we must remember that, at the time, this revelation was given, the Church was a year old and the members were a small group of farming families from the state of New York. They had few economic resources and little access to culture and secular knowledge. It is unthinkable that the first leaders could anticipate the future of the Church based only on their own experience and knowledge. Without a doubt, the revelation to Joseph Smith was from God, and today has witnessed its literal fulfillment:

> And also those to whom these commandments were given, might have power to lay the foundation of this church, and to bring it forth out of obscurity and out of darkness, the only true and living church upon the face of the whole earth, with which I, the Lord, am well pleased, speaking unto the church collectively and not individually. (D&C 1:30)

When enemies of the Church assassinated Joseph Smith and his brother Hyrum in 1844, they were convinced that Mormonism would ultimately disappear. That was not the case. Joseph played a central role in the restoration, but this is the Church of Christ, and members convert to Christ and not to their leaders.

In those days and also at the present time, the key still continues to be the same: individual and personal conversion to Christ. In 1829, when the Church was not yet organized, God told Joseph Smith:

> Remember the worth of souls is great in the sight of God; For, behold, the Lord your Redeemer suffered death in the flesh; wherefore he suffered the pain of all men, that all men might repent and come unto him.
> And he hath risen again from the dead that he might bring all men unto him, on conditions of repentance. (D&C 18:10-12)

A New Century 211

The atoning sacrifice of Jesus Christ is the central point of the gospel and Mormonism. All other aspects of the Church depend on this one: "I am the way, the truth, and the life: no man cometh unto the Father, but by me" (John 14:6).

This is the principal motive for the Church's missionary work over the past two centuries in this last dispensation.

What will happen to the Church in the future? It can only be glimpsed by what the apostles and prophets have declared. They hold the keys of revelation and the knowledge for all the Church. It is they who must be listened to in order to understand the instructions for future Church work and the role that each individual has within the gospel.

When the prophet speaks in the Church, his words have validity and application to each place, country, and nation. It was significant then, when our current prophet, President Gordon B.

Missionaries in Ushuaia, Argentina, a symbol of the Church's presence around the world.

Hinckley, met with members of the Church in Buenos Aires, Argentina on November 12, 1996. It was the largest meeting in the history of the Church: fifty thousand Saints.

Some of the words spoken by President Hinckley on that occasion shed light on the future of the Church in Argentina:

> Once we were a very small group. Now we are spread across the earth in one hundred sixty nations, 9.7 million strong, yet we are interested in one another as individuals. Each one of their problems is my problem. We are here to help them in any way possible.
>
> When this is accomplished it will be a great and significant day, a day of repentance, a day of resolutions, and a day to discontinue those things which we shouldn't do, as converts in "a holy nation" and as a people most "peculiar" (I Pet. 2:9), if we are not obedient to the Word of Wisdom, from this day forth we will be compliant.
>
> We believe in eternal marriage. If there are those here tonight that have not received the blessings of eternal marriage in the temple of the Lord then resolve now to do so and to decide from this day forward to do the things that make you worthy to go to his holy house. This privilege is a great and wonderful opportunity ....
>
> Let your families be families of love and peace and happiness. Gather your children around you and have your family home evenings, teach your children the ways of the Lord, read to them from the scriptures, and let them come to know the great truths of the eternal gospel as set forth in these words of the Almighty. If there be any among you who are not having family prayer, let that practice start now, to get on your knees together, if you can possibly do it, every morning and every evening and speak to the Lord and express your thanks. Invoke His blessings upon the needy of the earth, and speak to Him concerning your own well-being. I believe that God, our Eternal Father, will hear our prayers, and I urge you to have family prayers. Great blessings will come to your children if

A New Century 213

The choir in the Vélez Sarsfield Stadium, Buenos Aires.

President Hinckley with the stake presidents of Buenos Aires.

you will pray together, calling upon the Lord, expressing your thanks, and presenting before him the desire of your hearts.

I only mean to tell you that you are a great people. If you are trying to live the gospel of Jesus Christ, you are a great people. I desire to tell you how much I love you. This love is very real. I reach out to each of you. I would like to give every one of you an abrazo [hug], but I can't do it; there are too many of you.

I desire that all of you in this vast congregation remember that you have listened to Gordon B. Hinckley and to know that I know God lives. I know Jesus is the Christ our Savior, and our Redeemer.[1]

The invitation of President Hinckley to be a peculiar people seems to be one of the challenges of the coming decades,

But ye are a chosen generation, a royal priesthood, an holy nation, a peculiar people; that ye should shew forth the praises of him who hath called you out of darkness into his marvellous light: Which in time past were not a people, but are now the people of God: which had not obtained mercy, but now have obtained mercy. (1 Pet. 2:9–10)

When the Saints traveled to Zion, the Salt Lake Valley, they transformed from a culturally diverse group of settlers into a spiritually united people. Today, Saints have dispersed all over the world, living among different cultures, social levels, economic conditions, and political systems. The South American countries are culturally different from one another, with each nation having a defined and unique identity. The bonds of brotherhood in the Church stretch across nations and the prophet invites members of each country in South America to become one national driving force.

A New Century 215

Gordon B. Hinckley's meeting with fifty thousand church members in Buenos Aires, November 12, 1996.

By following this invitation, the Latter-day Saints will greatly contribute to the growth of the Church but they will also be loyal to their own nations, being good citizens and examples.

The local pioneers laid a faithful foundation for the work that has been done. Now the time has come in which the legacy that was received produces fruits and the gospel is proclaimed to each person.

Notes

1. Gordon B. Hinckley, *Liahona*, February 1997, 4.

Appendix A

HISTORICAL TIMELINE
PART I—BACKGROUND
1844–1922

1844	Jun 27	Joseph and Hyrum Smith are martyred in Carthage, Illinois.
1845	Sep 9	Leaders of the Church declare the intention to move west.
1846	Feb 4	Saints begin to emigrate out of Nauvoo. A ship named the *Brooklyn* sails from New York with a company of 238 Saints on course to the port of San Francisco.
	May 1	Dedication of Nauvoo Temple.
	Jul 29	Ship *Brooklyn* arrives in San Francisco.
	Sep 17	Last group of Saints leaves Nauvoo.
1847	Jul 22–24	Company of pioneers in which Brigham Young travels arrives in the Salt Lake valley.
	Jul 28	Brigham Young designates the site for the Salt Lake Temple.
	Dec 5	Brigham Young ordained as president of the Church.
1850–54		Missions organized in Scandinavia, France, Italy, Switzerland, Hawaii, India, Malta, Gibraltar, Germany, South Africa, and the Pacific Islands.
1851	Sep 5	Parley P. Pratt leaves on a mission to Chile.
	Nov 8	Missionaries arrive in Valparaíso.

	Nov 30	Phoebe Pratt, wife of Parley P. Pratt, gives birth to their son Omner in Valparaíso, Chile.
1852	Jan 7	Omner Pratt passes away.
	Jan 25	Missionaries moved to the city of Quillota.
	Mar 2	Missionaries return to Valparaíso, leave South America, and return to California.
1857	May 13	Parley P. Pratt, of the Quorum of the Twelve, is assassinated in Arkansas.
1857	Sep 11	Mountain Meadows Massacre takes place near Cedar City.
1857	Sep 15	Brigham Young declares martial law in Utah.
1860		Last handcart company arrives in Salt Lake valley.
1867		Salt Lake Tabernacle completed.
1869		Transcontinental railroad in Promontory, Utah is completed.
		Brigham Young Academy opens in Provo.
1876	Jan 7	First missionaries enter Mexico. Melíton G. Trejo is baptized and begins the translation of the Book of Mormon into Spanish.
1877	Aug 29	Brigham Young passes away.
1886		First edition of the Book of Mormon is published in Spanish.
1890	Sep 24	Wilford Woodruff publishes the manifesto indicating the cessation of polygamy.
1893	Apr 6	Salt Lake Temple is dedicated by Wilford Woodruff.
1898	Spring	First women missionaries set apart.
1898	Sep 13	Lorenzo Snow set apart as the fifth president of the Church.
1901	Aug 12	Heber J. Grant dedicates and establishes the mission in Japan.
1909		First Presidency issues the statement on the Origin of Man.
1916		Doctrinal Exposition on the Father and the Son is given.
1918	Oct 3	Joseph F. Smith receives the Vision of the Redemption of the Dead.

Historical Timeline 219

	Nov 23	Heber J. Grant is sustained and separated as president of the Church.
1919	Nov 27	Dedication of Hawaii Temple.

PART II—THE MISSIONS IN SOUTH AMERICA 1923–65

1923		Andrew Jenson (Assistant Church Historian) and Thomas S. Page visit South America.
	Aug 26	Dedication of Alberta Canada Temple.
1925		Heber J. Grant announces the beginning of the work in South America.
	Sep 4	First Presidency calls Melvin J. Ballard to the South America Mission.
	Oct 8	First Presidency separates Melvin J. Ballard, Rulon S. Wells, and Rey L. Pratt as South America missionaries.
	Dec 25	Melvin J. Ballard dedicates South America for the preaching of the gospel.
1926	Jan 14	Rulon S. Wells returns to the United States due to illness. In Buenos Aires the missionaries rent Rivadavia 8972 for meetings; considered the first mission house and is used for baptisms, with the first baptism being Eladia Cifuentes of Argentina.
	Jun 6	Second president to the South America Mission, Reinhold Stoof and his wife arrive in Buenos Aires.
	Jul 23	Elders Ballard and Pratt return to the United States.
1927	Sep 10	Mission house is moved from Rivadavia 8972 to Habana 3330.
1928		Church purchases Hill Cumorah.
1930	Nov 13	President Stoof and Elders Bluth and Wheeler travel to Rosario in the Argentina Republic. The work begins with the rental of San Juan 3548.
1933	Dec 28	J. Reuben Clark visits Montevideo and attends the Liniers Branch, Buenos Aires.

1935		South America Mission is divided, creating the Brazil and Argentina Missions.
	Aug 22	Stoof family returns to the United States. W. Ernest Young presides over the Argentina Mission.
	Dec 28	Work begins in La Plata, Argentina.
1936	Apr	Welfare plan is introduced in the Church.
1938	Aug 22	W. Ernest Young finishes his first mission in Argentina. Frederick S. Williams is new president of the Argentina Mission.
1939	Feb 9	Liniers Chapel at the corner of Tolenero and Cañada de Gómez is dedicated. First missionary from Argentina leaves to the mission field—Luis Constantini.
	Aug 24	Missionaries are evacuated from Europe before the imminent outbreak of the war.
1941	Apr 6	First Presidency announces a new position at the general level—assistant to the Twelve.
1942	Aug 1	James L. Barker arrives in Buenos Aires to preside over the Argentina Mission.
1944	Jun 25	Montevideo Branch is organized.
	Sep	W. Ernest Young returns to preside over the Argentina Mission for the second time.
1945	May 14	Heber J. Grant passes away.
	May 21	George Albert Smith is sustained as president of the Church.
1946		New missionaries in Argentina after World War II.
1947		Uruguay Mission is organized with Frederick S. Williams as president.
1948	Feb 3	Stephen L. Richards of the Quorum of the Twelve visits the Argentina Mission.
	Feb 27	Argentina mission house is moved to Virrey del Pino 2130, Belgrano, Buenos Aires.
1949		W. Ernest Young finishes his mission and is replaced by Harold Brown as president.
1951		David O. McKay is called to replace George Albert Smith as president.

1952		Lee B. Valentine replaces Harold Brown as president of the Argentina Mission.
1954	Jan 2	David O. McKay begins a tour of London, South Africa, South America, and Central America.
	Feb 3	President McKay meets with the president of Argentina, Juan D. Perón.
	Feb 7	Conference is held in the Teatro Nacional Cervantes.
	Feb 8	President McKay leaves for Santiago, Chile.
1955	April	Publication *El Mensajero Deseret* in the Argentina Mission is replaced by the magazine *Liahona*.
	Jun	Lee B. Valentine travels to Chile to initiate the work in Santiago.
	Dec 30	First meeting of the Church in La Plata.
1956	Jul 5	First branch of the Church in Santiago, Chile is organized.
	Aug 29	Lorin N. Pace replaces Lee B. Valentine as president in the Argentina Mission.
1959	Jan 21	Spencer W. Kimball visits the Argentina Mission. Andes Mission is created, with seat in Santiago, Chile, and J. Vernon Sharp as president.
1960		The chapel construction program is established, based on the missionary progress in the area.
	Oct 21	Organization of the first Directive Council of the Argentina Mission. C. Laird Snelgrove is the new president of the Argentina Mission.
	Nov 15	Joseph F. Smith visits the Argentina Mission accompanied by A. Theodore Tuttle.
1961		A. Theodore Tuttle becomes mission director of South America.
	Apr	Construction finishes on the Caseros Chapel.
1962	Sep 16	North Argentina Mission is organized with Ronald V. Stone as president.
1963	Jan	Hugh B. Brown visits the Saints in Argentina. Arthur H. Strong presides over the Argentina Mission.
	Aug	A. Theodore Tuttle meets with Argentina President Arturo Illia.

1964		Monday night is designated as Family Home Evening program night. Richard G. Scott replaces Ronald V. Stone in the Argentina North Mission.

PART III—THE STAKES OF ZION
1966–77

1966		Rex N. Terry presides over the Argentina Mission. Richard Evans and Franklin D. Richards visit the Argentina Mission.
May 1		First stake in South America is organized in São Paulo, Brazil.
Nov 20		Buenos Aires Stake is organized with Angel Abrea[1] as president.
1967	Mar	*Liahona* is published in Spanish.
	Sep 29	Regional representatives of the Twelve announce sixty-nine new missionary positions in the Church.
	Nov 12	Stake organized in Montevideo, Uruguay with Vicente Rubio as president.
1969		First LDS missionaries enter Spain.
1970	Jan 18	David O. McKay passes away.
	Jan 23	Joseph Fielding Smith is called as president of the Church with Harold B. Lee and N. Eldon Tanner as counselors.
	Jul 1	Spain Mission is organized.
1971	Aug 27–29	First Area Conference in Manchester, England. Seminary program begins in Argentina, Uruguay, and Paraguay. Church membership exceeds three million. *Ensign*, *New Era*, and *Friend* magazines launched.
1972	Jan	Program for future elders replaces the adult Aaronic Priesthood program.
	Feb 28	Stake organized in Córdoba with Arturo Palmieri as president.
	Mar 1	Stake organized in Mendoza with Mario A. Rastelli as president.

Historical Timeline 223

	Jul 2	Joseph Fielding Smith passes away. Harold B. Lee is called as president of the Church with N. Eldon Tanner and Marion G. Romney as counselors. Argentina Mission is divided with the Argentina North Mission being created and Joseph T. Bentley as president.
1973	Dec 26	Harold B. Lee passes away. Spencer W. Kimball is called as president of the Church with N. Eldon Tanner and Marion G. Romney as counselors.
1974		Church challenged to "lengthen its stride."
	May	Stake in Buenos Aires is divided with the Buenos Aires West Stake being created. Hugo A. Catrón and Juan A. Walker called as presidents.
1975	Mar	First Area General Conference in Buenos Aires for members of Argentina, Chile, Paraguay, and Uruguay. Spencer W. Kimball announces the construction of the São Paulo Temple in Brazil.
	Apr 3	General Conference supports inclusion of Joseph Smith's revelation on the celestial kingdom and Joseph F. Smith's revelation on the Vision of the Redemption of the Dead in the Pearl of Great Price.
1976	Apr	Seville Hugo is called to preside over the Spain Mission.
	Jul	Gene R. Cook presides over the Uruguay Mission in Montevideo.
	Oct 1	Assistants of the Twelve are called to be members of the First Quorum of the Seventy.
	Oct 3	Organization of the First Quorum of the Seventy is announced. Two revelations are added to standard works.
		Missionary Training Center opens in Provo.
1977		Paraguay Mission is organized with Merle Bair[2] as president.
	Oct 26	Announcement of construction of the Orson Hyde Commemorative Park at the Mount of Olives, Israel.

PART IV—TEMPLES
1978–84

1978	Jun 1	Spencer W. Kimball announces the revelation in which the blessings of the priesthood are granted to worthy men of all races.[3]
	Oct 26–27	Area General Conference in Montevideo.
	Oct 28–29	Area General Conference in Buenos Aires.
	Oct 30	President Kimball dedicates the São Paulo Brazil Temple.
	Dec 15	Helvecio Martins[4] is called to serve in the Stake Presidency in Brazil.
1979	Feb 25	First stake organized in Asunción, Paraguay with Carlos Espínola as president.
1981	April 4	Angel Abrea of Argentina is called to the First Quorum of the Seventy.
1982	April 1	Worldwide Church membership exceeds five million.
	Sep 11	Groundbreaking ceremony for the Lima Peru Temple.
1983	Sep 15	Gordon B. Hinckley dedicates the Santiago Chile Temple.
	Dec. 2	Dedication of Mexico City Mexico Temple.
1984	Apr 7	Construction of the Bogotá Columbia Temple is announced.
	Jun 24	First Presidency announces the concept of Area Presidencies.
	Jul	Members of the South America Area Presidency arrive in South Buenos Aires—A. Theodore Tuttle, Jacob de Jager, and Spencer H. Osborn.
	Aug	Boyd K. Packer and Bruce R. McConkie are called to the office of Buenos Aires Area Presidency.

PART V—WATCHING THE FUTURE
1985–2002

1985	Jul	J. Thomas Fyans is the new president of South America South Area.

Historical Timeline 225

	Aug 16	Angel Abrea arrives in Buenos Aires to preside over the Buenos Aires Temple.
	Nov 5	Spencer W. Kimball passes away.
	Nov 10	Ezra Taft Benson is called as president of the Church with Gordon B. Hinckley and Thomas S. Monson as counselors.
	Dec	Buenos Aires Temple open house.
1986	Jan 10–17	Dedication of Lima Peru Temple.
	Jan 17	Thomas S. Monson dedicates the Buenos Aires Temple.
	Jan 20	First baptismal service in the Buenos Aires Temple.
	Feb 6	Buenos Aires Missionary Training Center opens with Lyman Shreeve as president.
	Aug	Ted E. Brewerton is the new counselor to the Area Presidency.
	Oct 4	Stake Quorum of the Seventy is discontinued.
1987	Apr	Waldo P. Call is called as area president with John H. Groberg and L. Aldin Porter as counselors.
	Jul	Brothers Tomás F. Lindheimer and Carlos E. Agüero[5] are called as mission presidents.
1988	Jul	Carlos Espínola of Asunción, Paraguay is called to preside over the Ilamado, Chile Mission.
	Aug	The Church reaches one billion baptisms for the dead.
1989	Apr	Second Quorum of the Seventy is created. The leaders of the Church in Buenos Aires meet separately with three Argentina Presidential candidates—Eduardo Angeloz, Alvaro Alsogaray, and Carlos Menem.
1990	Apr	Eduardo Ayala of Chile and Helvecio Martins of Brazil are called to the Second Quorum of the Seventy.
	Jul 1	Argentina Missions of Mendoza, Trelew, and Resistencia are organized.
	Oct 1	Jacob de Jager is called as area president with Lynn A. Mickelsen and Eduardo Ayala[6] as counselors.
1991	Jun 24	Russia grants formal recognition to the Church.

	Sep 1	Membership of the Church reaches eight million.
1992	Feb 15	Groundbreaking ceremony for the Buenos Aires Missionary Training Center and Hostal del Templo.
	Oct 16	Uruguay President Dr. Luis Alberto Lacalle speaks to the young people at the Religion Institute in Montevideo. Lynn A. Mickelsen is called as area president with Horacio A. Tenorio and John B. Dickson as counselors.
1993	Dec	New edition of the triple combination writings including topical index is published in Spanish
1994	May 30	Ezra Taft Benson passes away.
	Jun 5	Howard W. Hunter is separated as fourteenth president of the Church with Gordon B. Hinckley and Thomas S. Monson as counselors.
1994	Dec 11	Two thousandth stake in the Church is created in Mexico.
1995	Jan	Church membership reaches nine million members. Announcement of temples in Cochabamba, Bolivia and Recife, Brazil.
	Mar 3	Howard W. Hunter passes away. Gordon B. Hinckley is called as president with Thomas S. Monson and James E. Faust as counselors.
	Apr	Area Authorities announce the call of regional representative and discontinuance of Administrative Church Regions.
	Aug 10	Groundbreaking ceremony for the Guayaquil Ecuador Temple.
	Aug 15	Area Presidency is reorganized with John B. Dickson called as president and F. Melvin Hammond and Hugo A. Catrón as counselors.
1996	April 6	Francisco J. Viñes is called to the Second Quorum of the Seventy.
	Nov 12	Gordon B. Hinckley meets with fifty thousand Saints in Buenos Aires.
	Aug	Gordon B. Hinckley visits Uruguay and Paraguay.

Historical Timeline 227

	Sep	Carlos H. Amado is called as president of South America South Area with Richard D. Allred and Hugo A. Catrón as counselors.
1999	Mar 6	Dedication of Colonia Juárez Chihuahua México Temple.
	Apr 24	Dedication of Bogotá Colombia Temple.
	Aug 1	Dedication of Guayaquil Ecuador Temple.
2000	Feb 26	Dedication of Ciudad Juárez Mexico Temple.
	Feb 27	Dedication of Hermosillo Sonora Mexico Temple.
	Mar 11	Dedication of Oaxaca Mexico Temple.
	Mar 12	Dedication of Tuxtla Gutiérrez Mexico Temple.
	Apr 30	Dedication of Cochabamba Bolivia Temple.
	May 20	Dedication of Tampico Mexico Temple.
	May 21	Dedication of Villahermosa Mexico Temple.
	Jul 8	Dedication of Mérida Mexico Temple.
	Jul 9	Dedication of Veracruz Mexico Temple.
	Aug 20	Dedication of Caracas Venezuela Temple.
	Dec 15	Dedication of Recife Brazil Temple.
	Dec 17	Dedication of Porto Alegre Brazil Temple.
2001	Mar 18	Dedication of Montevideo Uruguay Temple.
	Apr 29	Dedication of Guadalajara Mexico Temple.
2002	Apr 28	Dedication of Monterrey Mexico Temple.
	May 17	Dedication of Campinas Brazil Temple.
	May 19	Dedication of Asunción Paraguay Temple.
	Aug 23	Construction of Curitiba Brazil Temple.
2007	May 23	Construction of Manaus Brazil Temple.

Notes

1. Angel Abrea grew up as a Church member when Latter-day Saints were a rarity in his country. There were perhaps four hundred members of the Church in Argentina when he was baptized at age ten, in November of 1943. But years of Church experience, combined with parental support, molded Angel Abrea into the kind of individual who could be a counselor in the district pres-

idency at seventeen, and a branch president at twenty-three. He was later a district president, first stake president in his country, regional representative, and mission president before he was sustained as a member of the First Quorum of the Seventy on 4 April 1981. Searle, "Elder Angel Abrea," 25.

2. There is a little village called Mistolar in the Paraguayan desert. All of its residents are members of The Church of Jesus Christ of Latter-day Saints. Despite their distance from the Church's Paraguayan headquarters in the capital city of Asunción, these humble people of Indian ancestry follow the programs and principles of the restored gospel and are an example of faithfulness to the world. Mistolar had its beginnings in 1977. At that time the Paraguayan Mission President, Merle Bair, saw Walter Flores, a man from the deserts of the Chico in Paraguay, on a television program in Asunción. President Bair felt impressed to find the man and share the gospel with him. In 1980 the missionaries located Flores. He was very receptive to the gospel message and was soon baptized. Brother Flores' testimony was so profound and clear, he knew he had to share the gospel with his fellow Indians. Several hundred joined the Church. Ted E. Brewerton, "Mistolar: Spiritual Oasis," *Tambuli* (September 1990): 11.

3. A little more than a year later, in June 1978, we received a telephone call from a friend in Salt Lake City, Utah, telling us that President Kimball had announced the revelation that all worthy males could hold the priesthood. I shall not forget that day. My wife cried. I cried. We knelt to thank our Heavenly Father. After that, the phone rang many, many times. Friends from the United States and Brazil called us. Janet Peterson and Helvecio Martins, "Friend to Friend," *Friend* (January 1992): 6.

4. During the cornerstone laying of the São Paulo Temple, President Spencer W. Kimball motioned for me to come to him. I looked around to see whom he was looking at. He repeated the gesture. I did not understand. James E. Faust looked at me and mouthed "come here. He wants to talk to you." I went. President Kimball shook my hand and took hold of my arm and said, "Brother, what is necessary for you is faithfulness. Remain faithful, and you will enjoy all the blessings of the Church." Peterson and Martins, "Friend to Friend," 6.

5. This emphasis on education and missions is paying off in Buenos Aires. "In the past it was not common to see young men serve missions," says Area Authority Seventy Carlos E. Agüero. "We are seeing change with the generations. Now young men and women are going by the hundreds. Education and mission goals are becoming the new tradition for Latter-day Saint youth." Olsen, "Argentina's Bright and Joyous Day," 32.

6. I grew up in Coronel, Chile. When I was seven years old, I memorized a poem of fourteen verses and recited it before an audience of twelve hun-

dred people. After that experience I developed an increased desire to read more. I read about four little books a week. At that time my mother gave me a Bible. When I was twelve I read the Bible in about ten months. I was impressed with the history of the Old Testament and with the Atonement of the Savior in the New Testament. All my life I tried to find another book of scripture that would teach me more about these things. Janet Peterson and Eduardo Ayala, "Friend to Friend," *Friend* (March 1996): 6.

ORAL HISTORIES

Interviews by Néstor Curbelo were recorded on audio and video cassette and are filed in the Buenos Aires Church Office and in the Church Historical Department in Salt Lake City.

Name	City	Country	Year
Miguel Angel Avila	Buenos Aires	Argentina	1978
Robert P. Antonietti	Buenos Aires	Argentina	1978
Eric Karl Fischer	Mercedes	Argentina	1978
Iris M. & Lloyd Spannaus	Buenos Aires	Argentina	1978
Manuel Prieto	Rosario	Argentina	1988
Jaime Moltó	Mendoza	Argentina	1989
Alberto Emilio Steiner	Mendoza	Argentina	1989
María Elena Castro Steiner	Mendoza	Argentina	1989
Agustín Cano	Mendoza	Argentina	1989
Osvaldo Decoud	Asunción	Paraguay	1989
Walter Flores	Asunción	Paraguay	1989
Jorge Arenas	Mistolar	Paraguay	1989
Julio Yegros	Mistolar	Paraguay	1989
Maximiliano García	Trelew	Argentina	1989
Oscar D. Filipponi	Trelew	Argentina	1989
Jorge E. Detlefsen	Trelew	Argentina	1989

Noemí Hughes-Torres	Trelew	Argentina	1989
Eloisa Underwood-Williams	Gaiman	Argentina	1989
Alba Iris Romero	Durazno	Uruguay	1989
Luis Alberto Ferrizo	Flores	Uruguay	1989
María Renee Guex	Florida	Uruguay	1989
Ofelia Saavedra	Durazno	Uruguay	1989
Luis Alberto Pintos	Santa Lucía	Uruguay	1989
Cícero Vicente	Santa Lucía	Uruguay	1989
Cristino Rodríguez	Isla Patrulla	Uruguay	1990
Carmen Scholz	Cordova	Argentina	1990
Ricardo Scholz	Cordova	Argentina	1990
Juan Aldo Leone	Cordova	Argentina	1990
Tom Teubner Dolores	Cordova	Argentina	1990
Luka Ortlieb	Roque S. Peña	Argentina	1990
Rubén Morresi	Usuahia	Argentina	1990
Gustavo Romeu	Usuahia	Argentina	1990
Enrique Reyes	Río Grande	Argentina	1990
Juan Isidoro Rojo	Usuahia	Argentina	1990
Juana N. Galeano	Río Grande	Argentina	1990
Domingo Antonio González	Río Grande	Argentina	1990
Guillermo Flores	Bmé. de las Casas	Argentina	1990
Alejandro Peynoso	Bmé. de las Casas	Argentina	1990
Raúl Coglan	Formosa	Argentina	1990
Jeffrey D. Brown	Cte. Fontana	Argentina	1990
Michael J. Witchurch	Cte. Fontana	Argentina	1990
Avelino Juan Rodríguez	Montevideo	Uruguay	1991
Alfred H. Baker	San José	Uruguay	1991
Hugo Lomando	San José	Uruguay	1991
Heber Omar Díaz	Monte Crande	Argentina	1991
Ricardo García Silva	Santiago	Chile	1991
Max & Amy Willis	Santiago	Chile	1991

Oral Histories 233

Eunice & Hugh Maelor Hughes	Trelew	Argentina	1991
Perla Z. García	Santiago	Chile	1991
Harry Lockling Pieper	Santiago	Chile	1991
Eduvigis Daza	Viña del Mar	Chile	1991
Armondo Solis	Viña del Mar	Chile	1991
W. Craig Zwick	Santiago	Chile	1991
Holbrock Dupont	Santiago	Chile	1991
H. Clay Gorton	Santiago	Chile	1991
Vicente Rubio	Montevideo	Uruguay	1991
Sacramento Viñas	Montevideo	Uruguay	1991
Rafael Viñas	Montevideo	Uruguay	1991
James Wilson	Buenos Aires	Argentina	1991
Lloyd H. Richmond	Buenos Aires	Argentina	1991
Beatriz María Hillpes-Quintana	Neuquén	Argentina	1993
Robert E. Wells	Buenos Aires	Argentina	1997
César Guerra	Montevideo	Uruguay	1997
Desiderio Arce	Salta	Argentina	1998
González Family	Salta	Argentina	1998
Delia Ariki	Jujuy	Argentina	1998
Marks Huntemilla	Gral. Roca	Argentina	1999
Pedro Antonio & Teresa Sandoval-López	Gral. Roca	Argentina	1999
Héctor Daniel Huerta	Neuquén	Argentina	1999
Diógenes Martínez	Quiriza	Bolivia	1999
Luis A. Ramirez	Asunción	Paraguay	2000
Liduvina Sanchez-Nieves	Asunción	Paraguay	2000

BIBLIOGRAPHY

Acevedo, Rodolfo. *Los Mormones en Chile: 30 años de la Iglesia de Jesucristo de los Santos de los Últimos Días (1956–1986).* Santiago: Imprenta Cumora, 1990.
Alvarez, José Pedro. Manuscript. 1985.
"Argentina." http://www.lonelyplanet.com/destinations/south_america/argentina/index.htm (accessed June 22, 2006).
"Argentina." Vantage Adventures. http://www.travelvantage.com/argen.html (accessed June 22, 2006)
Argentina Mission Presidents. *History of the Argentina Mission.* 1925–53.
Avila, Ramón. Manuscript.
Balderas, Eduardo. "Northward to Mesa," *Ensign.* September 1972, 30.
Ballard, Melvin J. "The Three Degrees of Glory," *Sermons and Missionary Services of Melvin Joseph Ballard.* Salt Lake City: Deseret News Press. 1922, 10.
———. *Crusader for Righteousness.* Salt Lake City: Bookcraft, 1966.
———. "Dedication Prayer on South America," *South American Mission History*, vol II. December 25, 1925. LDS Church Historian's Office.
Ballard, M. Russell. "The Kingdom Rolls Forth in South America." *Ensign.* May 1986, 12.
Berrett, William E. "Church Education System (CES)," *Encyclopedia of Mormonism*, edited by Daniel H. Ludlow. Vol. 1. New York: Macmillan Publishing Company, 1992.
Brewerton, Ted E. "Mistolar: Spiritual Oasis," *Tambuli.* Sept. 1990, 11.

Bushman, Claudia Lauper, and Richard Lyman Bushman. *Building the Kingdom: A History of Mormons in America*. New York: Oxford University Press, 1999.
Christian, Lewis Earl. *Sandstone, Blackrock, and a Few Other Solid Matters: The Story of My Life*. 1979.
Church Educational System. *Church History in the Fulness of Times*. Salt Lake City: The Church of Jesus Christ of Latter-day Saints, 2000.
Conference Report. Salt Lake City: The Church of Jesus Christ of Latter-day Saints, semi-annual.
"Creole." Encyclopedia Britanica. Encyclopedia Britanica Premuim Service. http://www.britannica.com/eb/article?eu=28289 (accessed June 22, 2006)
Davies, Douglas James. *Mormon Spirituality: Latter Day Saints in Wales and Zion*. Nottingham, Eng.: University of Nottingham, 1987.
Deseret Morning News 2004 Church Almanac. Salt Lake City: Deseret Morning News, 2004.
El Mensajero Deseret. 1939–54.
Ensign. 1972–2004.
Erbolato, Flavia García. "The Church in Brazil," *Ensign*, February 1975, 24.
Family of Helaman Pratt, The. http://helaman.pratt-family.org (accessed June 22, 2006).
Flake, Joel Alva. "The History of the Church of Jesus Christ of Latter-day Saints in South America." M.A. thesis, Brigham Young University, 1975.
Friend. 1987–96.
Gianfelice, Antonino. Manuscript. Buenos Aires, 1985–86.
Grover, Mark L. "Mormonism in Brazil: Religion and Dependency in Latin America." Ph.D. diss., Indiana University, 1985.
———. "The Miracle of the Rose and the Oak in Latin America," edited by Susan E. Black, et. al. In *Out of Obscurity: The Church in the Twentieth Century*. Salt Lake City: Deseret Book, 2000, pp. 138-150.

Haight, David B. "Planting Gospel Seeds of Spirituality," *Ensign*. January 1973, 74.
———. "Special Witness: To Save Our Ancestors," *Friend*, August 2002, 7.
Hanks, Marion D. "Elder Richard L. Evans: Apostle of the Lord (1906–1971)," *Ensign*, December 1971, 2.
Haroldsen, Edwin O. "Elder Charles Didier," *Tambuli*, September 1988, 17.
Hatch, Nelle Spilsbury and B. Carmon Hardy, eds. *Stalwarts South of the Border.* El Paso, Tex.: Western College Press, 1985.
Herrera, Agricol Lozano. *Historia del Mormonismo en Mexico.* Mexico City: Editorial Zarahemla, 1983.
Himnos de la Inglesia de Jesucristo de los Santos de los Ultimos Dias. Salt Lake City: The Church of Jesus Christ of Latter-day Saints, 1993.
Hinckley, Bryant S. *Sermons and Missionary Services of Melvin Joseph Ballard.* Salt Lake City: Deseret Book, 1949.
Hinckley, Gordon B. "A Sacred Responsibility," *Tambulilit*. May 1992, 9.
Hymns of the Church of Jesus Christ of Latter-day Saints. Salt Lake City: The Church of Jesus Christ of Latter-day Saints, 1985.
Iverson, Steven J. "Chile," *Ensign*, February 1977, 44.
Ivins, H. Grant. "Polygamy in Mexico as Practiced by the Mormon Church, 1895–1905." Heber Grant Ivins Papers, 1910–74. Utah State Historical Society, Salt Lake City.
Jenson, Andrew. *South American Mission History*, Vol II. (December 6, 1925– February 26, 1926. LDS Church Historians Office.
———. *Encyclopedic History of The Church of Jesus Christ of Latter-day Saints*. Salt Lake City: Deseret News Publishing, 1941.
"Juan Lavalle," *The Columbia Electronic Encyclopedia*, 6th ed. New York: Columbia University Press, 2001.
Kimball, Spencer W. *Go to All the World*, transcription from the film.
Knell, Rulon. "History of Pinto, Utah," Library of Congress, Manuscript Division, WPA Federal Writers' Project Collection.

Knowles, Eleanor. *Deseret Book Company: 125 Years of Inspiration, Information, and Ideas.* Salt Lake City: Deseret Book Company, 1991.

Lindheimer, Tom S F. "The Church in Southern South America." *Encyclopedia of Mormonism.* New York: Macmillan Publishing company (1992). http://www.lightplanet.com/mormons/daily/history/south_america.html#ssa (accessed June 22, 2006).

Livingston, Craig. "'They are our Brothers': High Mormon Officials Respond to the Mexican Revolution, 1910–1917." M.A. thesis, Princeton University, 1999.

Maritime Heritage Project, The. http://www.maritimeheritage.org (accessed June 22, 2006).

Martin, David. *Tongues of Fire: The Explosion of Protestantism in Latin America.* London: Basil Blackwell, 1990.

McAllister, Jack. "The Unlikely Daniel Webster Jones: First Spanish Translations from the Book of Mormon," *Ensign*, August 1981, 50.

McConkie, Bruce R. "Prayer of Dedication on the Buenos Aires Temple Ground," *Liahona*, October 1983, 4.

⸺. quoted in "Groundbreaking for 4th temple in South America," *Church News*, May 1983, 4.

Mintz, S. "Digital History: Using new technologies to enhance teaching and research." *Italian Immigration* http://www.digitalhistory.uh.edu/historyonline/italian_immigration.cfm? (accessed June 22, 2006).

Olsen, Judy C. "Argentina's Bright and Joyous Day," *Ensign*. February 1998, 36.

Our Heritage: A Brief History of The Church of Jesus Christ of Latter-day Saints. Salt Lake City: The Church of Jesus Christ of Latter-day Saints, 1996.

Palmer, A. Delbert, and Mark L. Grover. "Hoping to Establish a Presence: Parley P. Pratt's 1851 Mission to Chile." Brigham Young University Studies, issue 38, no. 4 (1999): 115

Palmieri, Arturo. "Dangerous Times." *Ensign*, February 1977, 84.

Peterson, John De Leon Peterson. "History of the Mormon Missionary Movement in South America to 1940." M.A. thesis, Brigham Young University, 1961.
Phelps, WIlliam W. "Praise to the Man." http://mldb.byu.edu/phelps4.htm (accessed June 22, 2006).
Pratt, Parley P. Jr., *Autobiography of Parley P. Pratt*. Salt Lake City: Deseret Book Company, 1994 printing.
Roberts, Brigham H. *Comprehensive History of the Church of Jesus Christ of Latter-day Saints.* Salt Lake City: Deseret Book Company, 1954 printing.
Searle, Don L. "Elder Angel Abrea: Prepared for a Life of Service," *Ensign*, October 1984, 25.
Sharp, J. Vernon. "Prophecy of Elder Ballard," Diary.
Smith, Joseph Fielding. *Essentials in Church History*, 26th ed. Salt Lake City: Deseret Book Company, 1973.
Smurthwaite, Michael B. "Socio-Political Factors Affecting the Growth of the Mormon Church in Argentina Since 1925." M.A. thesis, Brigham Young University, 1968.
Sonne, Conway B. *Saints on the Seas*. Salt Lake City: University of Utah Press, 1983.
Speakman, Marie Dean. "History of Parley Parker Pratt" http://www.gordonbanks.com/gordon/family/pppratt.html (accessed June 22, 2006).
Spencer, Gerry. "Dedication of South America for Gospel Commemorated." *Mormon News*. December 5, 2000.
Taylor, John. "A Period of Trials and Testing," *A Brief History of the Church of Jesus Christ of Latter-day Saints*. Salt Lake City: The Church of Jesus Christ of Latter-day Saints, 1996.
"The House of the Lord." http://www.lds.org/temples/home/0,11273, 1896-1,00.html (accessed June 22, 2006).
Todd, Jay M. "Harold Brown of Mexico City," *Ensign*. September 1972, 1.
Tullis, F. LaMond. *Mormonism in Mexico: The Dynamics of Faith and Culture*. Logan: Utah State University, 1987.
Tuttle, A. Theodore. "What Is a Living Prophet?" *Ensign*. July 1973, 18.

Tvedtnes, John A. "The 'Other Tribes': Which Are They?" *Ensign*, January 1982, 31.
Urugual Montevideo Mission History. http://www.asquared.com/inepub/URUMission/history/index.asp (accessed June 22, 2006).
Walker, Juan A. "So Many Prodigals," *Ensign*. Mar. 1979.
Whittaker, David J. "The Articles of Faith in Early Mormon Literature and Thought," *New Views of Mormon History, A Collection of Essays in Honor of Leonard J. Arrington*; Bitton, Davis and Maureen Ursenbach Beecher, eds. Salt Lake City: University of Utah Press, 1987.
Williams, Frederick S., and Frederick G. Williams. *From Acorn to Oak Tree: A Personal History of the Establishment and First Quarter Century Development of the South American Missions*. Fullerton, Calif.: Et Cetera Graphics, 1987.
Young, W. Ernest. Diary. 1973.

INDEX

A

Abad, Jorge O., 155, 160
Abrea, Angel, xviii, xx, xxi, xxivn1,145–50, 156–60, 176, 178, 200–205, 206n2, 206n4
Abrea, Edealo, 206
Abrea, María Victoria Chiapparino, 149–51, 181, 201, 206n4
Abrea, Oscar, 156, 160, 206
Abrea, Zulema Estrada, 201, 206
Acevedo, Rodolfo, 10
Africa, xi, 190
Agüero, Carlos E., xxi n 4,155, 203, 160
Aguilar, Daniel, 156
Alasia, Julio C., 160
Allen, Rufus, 3, 8, 12n8, 31
Allred, Jeffrey T., 197
Allred, Richard D., xxiii
Allred, Verle, 141n2
Alsogaray, Alvaro, xxii
Alta Gracia, Córdoba, 101
Alvarez, Daniel P., 160
Alvarez, José Pedro, 72, 74–75
Alvarez, Ramón, 156
Amado, Carlos H., xxiii, 193, 196, 203
Anderson, C. Dixon, 154
Andes, xvi, 84n9, 98, 136, 140–41,
Angeloz, Eduardo, xxii
Antonietti, Roberto Pedro., 72–74, 107–108, 215
Arce, Desiderio, 217
Arenales River, 126
Arenas, Jorge, 215

Argyle, Shane V., 154
Arias, María Catalina Paz, 53
Ariki, Angelica Honoria Yamada, 26
Ariki, Delia, 217
Arizona, 24, 28, 45, 66, 206; temple, 72, 164–65
Arraucanians, 5
Arroyito, Rosario, 113–14
Asia, 191
Ashton, Preston E., 45, 78
Articles of Faith, xxix, xxx, 80
Australia, 103
Austria, 206n2
Avila, Elisa Leonor Melga, 88–91
Avila, Francisco, 91
Avila, José Luis, 89–92
Avila, Juan Carlos, 91–92, 112–13, 117, 145–47, 155–59
Avila, Miguel Angel, 67–68, 91–92, 113–17, 147, 215
Avila, Ramón, 87–95
Ayala, Eduardo, xxii, xxivn5

B

Bagnati, Daniel, 178
Bahía Blanca, Buenos Aires, 60, 104–107, 156, 160
Baker, Alfred H., 216
Balderas, Eduardo, 28, 164, 166n3
Ball, Joseph, 17
Ballard, M. Russell, 206
Ballard, Melvin J. xiii, xxxii, 32–41, 45–47, 51, 55n7, 55n14, 65, 78, 136–37, 154, 183, 200, 202, 204
Banfield, Buenos Aires, 147, 180
Barjollo, Fermín C., 78–80, 102, 143, 200
Barker, James L., xiv, 76–77, 154
Baroni, David H., 156, 159
Baroni, Horacio, 144
Barrientos, Sister, 133
Beal, J. 12n8
Belgrano, Buenos Aires, 103, 127, 147, 203
Benson, Ezra Taft, xxi-xxii, 163, 180, 182
Bentley, Anthony, 154
Bentley, Joseph T., xix, 141n2, 156
Berta, Gustavo C., 154, 160
Bettilyon, Verden E., 154
Biébersdorf, Ernst, 33–35, 49
Biébersdorf, María Cziesla, 34–35
Bishop, Joseph L., Jr., 154
Blanc, Alfredo, 144
Blanchard, Brother, 21–22
Bluth, Gayle, 156
Bluth, Lothaire A., xiv, 53
Bolivia, 48, 120n4, 136–37, 140, 160, 172, 174n4, 186n2, 191, 201, 217
Bony family, 101
Borello, Osvaldo, 147
Boren, Clara Lorenzi, 206n2
Boren, Samuel, 71–72, 79, 141, 200, 206n2
Brazil, xiv, xviii-xx, xxi n2, 51, 57–82, 83n2, 83n4, 84n6, 84n7, 84n8, 121n4, 136,

141n1, 158, 169–73, 174n1, 174n3, 174n4, 186n2, 191
Brewerton, Ted E., xxi, 195
Brigham Young University, 22, 120n1
Brooklyn, xi
Brown, Harold, xv, 98, 111–15, 120n1, 153–54, 200
Brown, Hugh B., xvii, 103
Brown, J. 12n8
Brown, Jeffrey D., 216
Brown, Marvin E., 155
Brundage, Harry P., 45, 67
Burton, James, 108–109

C

Cabrera, Buenos Aires, 103
Call, Waldo P., xxi, 77, 178, 183, 187n8, 192, 195
Caminos, Juan José, 53
Canada, 186n2
Cano, Agustin, 215
Cano family, 74, 108
Cappi, Antonio R., 157, 203
Cardon, R. Lavor, 156
Carthage, Illinois, xi
Casaday, Patrick, 157
Caseros, Buenos Aires, xvii, 145–47
Castelar, Buenos Aires, 76
Castillo, Jorge L. del, 203
Catholic Church 11, 20, 48, 84n7, 165, 206n2
Catrón, Hugo A., xxiii, 128, 145–47, 159, 176, 178, 186, 196, 203
Cebrian, Praxedes, 128
Central America, 191, 201
Central Argentina Railroad, 78
Chaco, Argentina, 48, 84n9, 131
Chehda, Adrián, 128
Chehda, Faiel, 128
Chehda, Felisa Yamada, 126
Chelius, Brian D., 128, 128
Chile, xii, xvi, xix, xxivn5, xxxii, 3–14, 75, 136–40, 141n2, 152n1, 160, 172, 175–76, 191, 194, 197–98, 217
Christensen, Shirley Dean, 157
Christian, Lewis E., 45, 48, 55, 64, 78

Chubut Valley, 96–98, 100
Chumbita, Julio E., 160, 178, 187n7
Church Education System, 115, 117, 121, 126
Cifuentes, Eladia, 219
Cittadini, Juan Carlos, 147
Ciudadela, Buenos Aires, 89, 95
Clark, J. Reuben, xiv, 47, 52
Clarke, J. Richard, 197
Clegg, Heber M., 44–45, 52, 63, 78
Coals, Copper, 131
Coburn, Thomas, 156
Cocco, Jorge, 8
Coglan, Raúl, 232
Colombia, 136, 160, 172, 186n2, 191
Conde family, 129
Constantini, Luis, xiv, 72, 75
Córdoba, Argentina, 60, 76, 80, 101–103, 117, 123, 127, 147–48, 152, 155, 158–60, 200, 202
Coronel, Luis C., 157, 160
Correa, Hanako Yamada, 128
Costa Rica, 137, 191
Craven, Inés, 129
Craven, Ricardo, 131
Crockett, Ketih, 155
Cuevas, Juan C., 131
Cummings, Horacio, 25

D

Dahl, Lawrence T., Jr., 155
Davis, Paul W., 45
Davis, Rollin S., 155
Daza, Eduvigis, 217
Decoud, Osvaldo, 215
Detlefsen, Jorge E., 216
Díaz, Heber Omar, 147, 160, 166, 18, 217
Dickson, John B., xxii, xxiii, 193, 195, 203
Didier, Charles A., 176, 186n2
Dissidents Cemetery, 4, 6, 12n5
Dock Sud, Argentina, 33–35, 39
Doctrina y Covenios, 25–26, 31
Doctrines and Covenants, 25, 28, 83n5, 107, 161–62, 189–90, 209–11

Dolavon, Patagonia, 96
Dolores, Tom Teubner, 216
Dömrose, Albert Ludwing, 93–96
Dömrose children, 95
Dömrose, María Sophia, 93
Dorrego, Manuel, 121n4
Dracut 9, 12n8
Ducher, María, 53
Duke, Elder, 106
Dupont, Holbrock, 217

E

Echegaray, Juan, 156
Eastwood, Charles W., 157
Echesortu, Rosario, 53–54
Ecuador, 136, 172, 186n2, 191
El Salvador, 191
Emigration Canyon, 151
England, 120n1
Escudero, Carmen, 78
Esquel, Patagonia, 96
Europe, xvi, xxxi, 17, 38, 51, 87, 94, 159, 163, 165, 186n2, 190, 202, 206n4
Evangelio Restaurado, El, 31, 39, 42
Evans, Richard, xvii
Ezeiza, Argentina, 176

F

family home evening, xvii
Fausett, Grant C., 154
Faust, James E., xxiii, xxivn3 171, 226,
Fernández, Angel M., 127, 148, 156, 158–59, 200
Fernández, Carlos R., 155, 160
Ferrizo, Luis Alberto, 216
Fetzer, Emil, 171–73, 174n3
Filipponi, Oscar D., 216
Finlinson, E. Reece, 156
Fischer, Eric Karl, 50, 215
Flores, Guillermo, 216
Flores, Walter, 215
Floresta, Buenos Airesm 112, 115, 147
Folson, Sister, 137
Fotheringham, William, 137,

Index 243

141n2
France, xi, 5, 20–21, 120n4
Franco, José Carlos, 145
Friedrichs, Minna Fredericka, 34
Friedrichs, Wilhelm, 32–34, 42
Frol, Ireneo, 155, 159
Fyans, J. Thomas, xx, 178, 183, 192, 195

G

Gabasa, Claribel, 181, 187n6
Gabasa, Egeo A., 147, 181, 187n6
Gaiman, Patagonia, 96
Gaivota, A, 84
Galeano, Juana N., 216
Galmes, Carlos Rinaldo, 129
Gambarotto, Isabel, 181
Gambarotto, Pablo L., 159, 178, 181
García, Enrique Manuel, 156
García, Maximiliano, 216
García, Perla Z., 217
Gardner, John B., 45
Gardner, Robert Q., 156
Gardner, Ron, 156
Garff, Louis, 14
Gavioli, Ramona Benita Arias, 53
Gazzoni, Hugo R., 147, 155, 159, 200
genealogy, 17, 151, 165–66
George, Richard R., 157
German, xi, 11, 32, 34, 38–39, 45–54, 55n7, 55n9, 55n14, 58, 62, 81, 83n1, 87, 93, 111–12, 136, 141n1, 190
Gianfelice, Antonino, 42–44, 71–76, 112, 144–45, 152n2, 200
Gianfelice children, 44
Gianfelice, Donato, 42, 68
Gibraltar, xi
Giuliani, Esteban, 141
González, Domingo Antonio, 216
González family, 233
Gorton, H. Clay, 103, 148, 155, 217
Grant, Heber J., 70, 164, xv

Green, P. Hap, 154
Groberg, John H., xxi
Guatemala, 191
Guerra, César, 217
Guex, María Renee, 216
Guiñazú, Argentina, 101
Guyana, 137, 186n2

H

Haedo, Buenos Aires, 72–75, 144
Hall, Rick, 155
Hall, Wendell H., 154–55
Hansen, Craig, 154
Harris, John Arthur, 154
Harvard University, 120n1
Heinz, William Fred, 45, 57
Henry Kelsey, 3, 12n2
Herrero, Francisco, 147
Hill, Craig A., 155
Hinckley, Gordon B., xxiii, 130, 167n3, 175, 180, 211–15
Holland, 15, 96, 93–94, 109n5, 191, 206n2
Holland, Gary, 178
Honduras, 191
Hong Kong, 191
Hoppe, Emil, 32–34, 61
Hoppe, Hildegard, 34
Hoppe, Sophia, 34
Houlin, Guillermo, 206n4
Houlin, James Patrick, 202, 206n4
Houlin, Patricia Abrea, 202, 206n4
Howells, Rulon S., 58, 83n4
Huerta, Héctor Daniel, 157, 217
Hughes, Eunice, 233
Hughes, Hugh Maelor, 217
Hugo, Seville, 217
Huntemilla, Marks, 217
Hunter, Howard W., xxii-xxiii 148
Hutchison, Richard C., 156

I

Ibarra, Enrique A., 147, 160, 178
Ikehara, Inocenia Berta Yamada, 128
Illia, Arturo, xvii
India, xv
Indians, 20, 28n3, 48, 228
Irish emigrants, 103
Israel, 9–10, 51, 70, 172
Italy, xi, 42, 74, 87–89, 103, 109n5, 159, 206n3
Ivins, Anthony W., 13, 15, 25, 29n9
Ivins, Antoine R., 164

J

Jager, Jacob de, xx, xxii 191–92, 197–98
Japan, 84n7, 191, 218
Jensen, Jewel C., 45, 63, 78
Jensen, M. Curtis, 156
Jenson, Andrew, xiii, xxxiin2,
Jones, Daniel W., 13, 22, 28n1
Jones, Evan, 101
Jones, Wiley C., 13
Jujuy, Argentina, 48, 100, 120n4, 217

K

Kaiser, Roland G., 68
Klein, O. James, 155
Kimball, Camilla, 127
Kimball, Spencer W., xvi, xix-xxi, xxivn2, xxivn3, 59, 127, 138, 145, 147, 165, 169–75, 199, 206
Korea, 191
Kullick, Anna Biébersdorf, 34–35
Kullick, Herta, 34–35
Kullick, Jacob, 34–35

L

Lacalle, Luis Alberto, xxii
Landowski, Paul, 84n6
Lamanites, 13, 38, 47–51, 70, 165
La Plata, Buenos Aires, xiv, xvi, 59, 72, 143, 145, 158, 200

Lanús, Argentina, 35, 39
Lara, Fernando A., 25
Latin America, xxix, xxxii, 25, 137, 171
Lavalle, Juan, 114, 120n4
Lázara, Ignacio, 144
Lazarte family, 129
Lee, Harold B., xviii, xix, 59, 115, 139–40,
Lencina, Edith Elisabeth Biébersdorf, 34–35
Lencina, Tato, 119, 120
Leone, Carlos, 101
Leone, Juan, 101
Leone, Juan Aldo, 100, 216
Leone, Líbara, 101
Lestani, Sister, 131–33
Liahona, xvi, xviii, 84
Libro de Mormón, 19, 32
Lindheimer, Tomás F., xxi, 147, 152n3, 155, 157, 160, 180
Liniers, Buenos Aires, xiv, 33, 39, 42, 52, 60, 67–78, 90–91, 112, 145
Lloyd, Paul, 104
Lomando, Hugo, 216
Loomis, J., 12n8
Looney, Agnes Mitchell, 103
Looney, María Angela Dido, 103, 105
Looney, Murti, 103
Looney, Thomas Murti, 103–107
Loper, Captain, 12
López, David, 203
López, Estanislao, 120n4
Lopez, M., 12n8
López, María, 89
López, Pedro Antonio, 217
López, Teresa Sandoval, 217
López, Wilfredo R., 157
Lord, R., 12n8
Lorenti family, 129
Los Delicias, Argentina, 53
Lozano, Agricol, 156
Lunt, Gary, 55
Lynn, Gerald O., 61, 69, 104
Lyon, Ted, 145

M

Macdonald, David M., 157
Madero, Francisco, 29n8
Maipu, Córdoba, 127
Malta, xi
Mar del Plata, Buenos Aires, 186
Martínez, Diógenes, 217
Martínez, Victor, 127
Martins, Helvecio, xx, xxivn2
Mazal, Roberto, 160
McConkie, Bruce R., xx, 176–79, 194, 197
McKay, David O., xv, xvi, xviii, 58, 84n7, 111, 115–20, 135–37, 141n2, 150, 165, 167n3
McKay, Robert, 118
Memmott, Fletcher, 77
Mendoza, Argentina, xviii, xxii, 73–75, 107–109, 147–48, 157
Menem, Carlos, xxi
Mensajero Deseret, El, xvi, 80, 85n25, 99, 100, 116–17
Mercurio, El, 11
Merlo, Buenos Aires, 73–74, 94, 96, 147, 149
Merrill, Douglas B., 45, 48, 55n15
Merrill, Hyde, 156
Merz, Sister, 129
Mexico, xii, xxii, xxxii, 13–28, 28n2, 29n8, 29n9, 29n11, 53, 59, 72, 120n1, 164, 171, 187n8, 191, 201
Michalek, Ricardo, 160
Mickelsen, Lynn A., xxii, 193, 195,
Mimosa, 96
Missionary Training Center, xix-xxii, 158
mission directive council, xvi 143–45
Moltó, Jaime, 215
Monroy, Carlos, 157
Monson, Thomas S., xxi-xxiii, 178, 180, 183
Montani, Inés Looney, 104, 106–107
Montani, Mario José, 107
Montani, Thomas, 107

Monte Grande, Buenos Aires, 217
Moore, Gary K., 155
Moreira, Sister, 99
Moreno, Daniel A., 160
Mormones in Chile, Los, 10
Morresi, Rubén, 216
Mortensen, Paul, 129
Moyle, Henry D., 59, 84n7, 138, 141n2, 163
Muren, Joseph C., 197

N

Nauvoo, Illinois, xi, xxxi, 17, 162
Neighbor, The, 11
Neuquén, Argentina, 157, 160, 217
New Zealand, 190
Nicaragua, 160, 191
Nieves, Liduvina Sanchez, 217
Notaro, Luigi, 44, 67–69
Notaro, María Antonia, 44, 67
Nueva Pompeya, Buenos Aires, 60, 91, 112

O

Ogden, Steven Dale, 156
Oguey family, 101
Olaiz, Robert, 145
Oliver, Allen B., 156
Oliver, Larry, 126, 128
Olsen, Eugene F., 152n1
Omill, María Rosario, 128–29
Ontiveros, Levi, 156
Oribe, Manuel, 120n4
Ortega, Fernando D., 160
Ortiz, Brother, 99
Ortlieb, Luka, 216
Osborn, Spencer H., xx, 178, 183, 193
Oveson, Stephen Berg, 155

P

Pace, Lorin N., 154, 221
Pacific, xi, 1–12, 17, 150, 190
Packer, Boyd K., xx, 178, 183, 194

Páez, Ramon, 178, 186n5
Page, Thomas S., xiii, xxxii, xxiiin2
Palmieri, Arturo, xviii, 147
La Pampa, Argentina, 84n9, 84n10
Panama, 191
Paraguay, xviii, xix 65, 136, 152n3, 160, 172, 174, 176, 186n2, 191, 194, 206n2, 215-217
Parisi, Salvador, 72
Parque San Martín, Buenos Aires, 74, 95–96
Parque Tres de Febrero, 33, 36–37
Párraga, María M. Biébersdorf, 34–35, 49
Patagonia, Argentina, 84n10, 96
Pearl of Great Price, 25–28, 83n4
Pecollo, Rosa, 107, 112
Pedersen, Eduardo, 178
Pedraja, Carlos Lizardo, 157
Pergamino, Buenos Aires, 59, 72, 76, 144
Perkins, Pastor, 108, 109
Perkins, Wayne C., 155
Peron, Eva Duarte (Evita), 120n4
Peron, Juan D.,117-18, 120n4, 206n2
Peru, 135–40, 151, 186n2
Peynoso, Alejandro, 216
Philippines, 21, 191, 193
Pieper, Harry Lockling, 217
Pina, Rafael Eduardo, 156
Pincock, Blair D., 157
Pintos, Luis Alberto, 232
Pitarch, Guillermo R., 156, 160
Plassman, Elisa, 34–35
Platt, Clair H., Jr., 126
Plural marriage, 15, 29n9
Poland, 93
Porter, L. Aldin, xxi, 97
Porter, Lanette, 97
Portuguese, 58, 83n5
Pratt, Helaman, 28n2
Pratt, McKay L., 107
Pratt, Omner, 5–7, 12n5, xii
Pratt, Parley P., xii-xiii, xxxii,
xxxiin2,1–12n8, 14, 17, 22, 32
Pratt, Phoebe Sopher, xii, 3, 5, 12n8, 31
Pratt, Rey L., xiii, xxxii, 16, 24–25, 32–33, 37–38, 45, 55n14, 137
Presbyterian, 12n11, 108-109
Prieto, Angel, 53
Prieto, Dorinda, 53, 114
Prieto, Hilda, 53
Prieto, Jorge, 160
Prieto, Manuel, 53, 215
Primary Children's Hospital, 151
Puerto Madryn, Patagonia, 96

Q

Quilmes, Argentina, 59, 81, 104, 107, 144, 147
Quintana, Beatriz María Hillpes, 217

R

Ramirez, Luis A., 217
Ramos, Alfonso, 155
Rastelli, Mario A., xviii, 147
Rawson, Chubut, 99
Record, Stephen C., 155
Rello, P., 12n8
Resistencia, Chaco, xxii 131–33, 157
Revelaciones del los Ultimos Dias, 25, 27
Reyes, Enrique, 216
Rhodacanaty, Plotino C., 29n11
Richards, Franklin D., xvii, 145
Richards, Stephen L, xvii, 58, 82–83, 103, 166n3
Richmond, Lloyd H., 155, 217
Righi, Omar R., 155, 159
Rio Cuartro, Córdoba, 80, 100
Rio de la Plata, 35–36
Rivera, Consulate, 107
Roberts, B. H., 17
Rodríguez, Avelino Juan, 216
Rodríguez, Cristino, 216
Rojo, Juan Isidoro, 216
Romero, Alba Iris, 101, 216
Romero, Cecilio Mario, 157
Romeu, Gustavo, 216
Romney, Marion G., xix, 171
Rosario, Santa Fe, xiv, xvi, 52–54, 59, 78, 102, 113, 120, 131, 143–44, 147, 156, 156–60, 163, 200
Rosas, Juan Manuel de, 120n4
Rossini, Emilia Farías, 129
Rovira, Raúl, 144
Rubalcava, Israel, 157
Rubio, Vicente, xviii, 217
Ryard, A., 12n8

S

Saavedra, Ofelia, 216
Saez, Gabriel, 203
Sagers, Harrison, 17
Saldívar family, 74
Salt Lake City, Utah, xii, xiii, xxiv n 2, xxxi, 1, 13–15, 21, 24–25, 38, 45, 65, 140, 145, 149–52, 180, 193, 201–202, 214
Salta, Argentina , 126–28, 131, 133, 156, 217
Salvioli, Hugo N., 77, 141, 143, 147, 156, 158, 160, 200
Sampson, C. E., 12n2
San Nicolás, Rios, 59, 200
Sangirgio, Lucía, 112
Santa Fe, Argentina, 80, 120n4
Sarmiento, Buenos Aires, 145
Schindler, Emil, 45, 57
Scholz, Carmen, 62, 64, 103, 216
Scholz, Ricardo, 62, 64, 103, 216
Schuck, Brian, 156
Scott, Richard G., xvi, 127, 140, 145, 153, 155
Sell, Adel, 57
Sell, Bertha, 57
Sell, Siegfried, 57
Sell, Theodore, 57
Sghimkat, Luis, 61
Sharp, J. Vernon, xvi, 37–38, 44–45, 48, 64, 83, 137, 140,
Shreeve, Lyman, xxi, 71
Sill, William, 128–29

Silva Costa, Heitor da, 84n6
Silva, Ricardo García, 217
Simpson, Robert L., 178, 183
Smith, George Albert, xv
Smith, Hyrum, xi
Smith, Joseph, xi, xxix-xxxi, 1, 17, 32, 47, 60, 97, 161, 182, 209–10
Smith, Joseph Fielding, xvii, xviii
Snelgrove, C. Laird, xvii, 76, 124, 143, 153–54
Snelgrove, Edna, 124
Solis, Armondo, 217
Sorensen, Asael T., 59
Sorensen, Gary, 157
Sorrento, Rosario, 53–54
Sorroza family, 129
Southest Asia, 191
Spain, xviii, 15, 17–20, 55n7, 55n14, 55n17, 84n11, 87, 108, 158–60, 186n1, 187n8, 206n3
Spannaus, Iris Myfanwym, 97, 215
Spannaus, Lloyd, 97, 215
Spencer, I. Russell, 45, 64, 78
Spitale, Paul, 156
Spitale, Rubén B. Luis, 157
Stay, Jesse E., 156
Steimle, W. Douglas, 157
Steiner, Alberto Emilio, 215
Steiner, María Elena Castro, 215
Stewart, George O., 157
Stewart, James Z., 13–14, 18, 22
Stoddard, Waldo I., 38, 44–45, 48, 57, 63, 183
Stone, Patricia J., 124
Stone, Ronald V., xvii, 124, 127, 155
Stoof, Ella, 37, 40, 64, 83n1
Stoof, Reinhold, xiii-xiv, 37–40, 45–53, 55n7, 57, 64, 68, 83n1, 131, 136, 141n1, 154
Strong, Arthur H., xvii, 99, 143, 152n1, 154, 158–59
Strong, Nedra Heward, 152n1
Sulé, Raquel, 165
Surinam, 186n2
Switzerland, xi, 52, 101, 103, 163

T

Taiwan, 191
Tandil, Buenos Aires, 114
Tanner, N. Eldon, xviii, xix
Taylor, John, 29n9
Teatro Nacional Cervantes, xvi, 117–20
Temple Inn, xxii
Tenorio, Horacio A., xxii, 195
Tenney, Ammon M., 13, 28n3
Terry, George, 14
Terry, Rex N., xvii, 143, 145, 154
Thatcher, Moses, 22, 29n11
Thomas, Gordon K., 157
Thompson, Mirta Demarchi, 165
Tidei, Rubén S., 155
Tigre, Buenos Aires, 61, 64
Transcontinental Railroad, 218
Torres, Noemí Hughes, 98, 216
Trejo, Antonio de, 20
Trejo, Don Pedro Fernando de, 18
Trejo, Emily Jones, 22
Trejo, Melitón González, 14, 18–24
Trelew, Argentina, 96–100, 157
Trozos Selectos del Libro de Mormón, 13, 22–23
Trozos Selectos Doctrina y Convenios, 31
Trumbull, David, 11–12n11
Tucumán, Argentina, 128–31
Turley, Marvin, E., 157
Tuttle, A. Theodore, xvii, xx, 72, 84n10, 123–24, 127,135, 150, 180, 191–94, 197, 200
Tuttle, Marné, 124, 127

U

Udall, David K., 154
Union Church, 11
University of Bordeaux, 20
University of Cuyo, 108
Uruguay, xv, xviii-xix, xxii, 52, 65, 72, 85n25, 120n1, 121, 123, 136, 152n3, 191, 186n2, 206n2, 216-217

V

Valentine, Lee B., xv-xvi, 115, 117–18, 137, 154
Valle 16 de Octubre, Patagonia, 96–97
Vazquez, Gerardo, 155
Venezuela, 136–37, 186n2, 191
Ventura, Jorge, 156, 203
Verdugo, Héctor M., 157
Vergelli, Emilio, 101–102, 144, 147, 157, 165
Vergelli, Laura, 101–102
Vicente, Cícero, 216
Vicente López, Buenos Aires, 147
Villarreal, Jerry R., 155
Viñas, Francisco J., 156
Viñas, Rafael, 217
Viñas, Sacramento, 217
Voice of Warning, A, 22

W

Wajchman, Luis, 156
Walker family, 104
Walker, Juan A., 147
Welfare plan, 54
Wells, Robert E., 98, 140, 176, 200, 217
Wells, Rulon S., xviii, 32–38, 55n9, 78, 219
Wheeler, Victor, 45, 53, 219
Widtsoe, John, 104
Wilkins, Alan Lee, 154
Wilkins, Ernest J., 68
Williams, Eloisa Underwood, 216
Williams, Frederick S., xiv, xv 42–45, 52, 60–72, 78–80, 101, 107, 36–37, 154, 200
Willis, Amy, 217
Willis, Max, 217
Wilson, James, 131–32, 217
Winn II, D. Clive, 154
Witchurch, Michael J., 217
Woodruff, A. O., 29n9
Woodruff, Willford, 29n9, 218
World War II, xv, 34, 58, 77, 80, 93, 102-103, 107, 109, 111, 113, 200

Y

Yamada, Tomie, 126
Yegros, Julio, 231
Young, Amy, 59
Young, Brigham, xi, xii, xxx, 5, 9, 14, 21–22, 151, 194
Young, Carl, 59, 77
Young, Cecile, 59
Young, W. Ernest, xiv, xv, 16, 59–61, 68, 77–83, 85n11, 85n25, 154, 180, 206n2
Young, Walter, 59

Z

Zaldivar family, 108
Zappey, Cornelius, 94–95, 109n5
Zwick, W. Craig, 217

Also available from
GREG KOFFORD BOOKS

The Trek East: Mormonism Meets Japan, 1901–1968

Shinji Takagi

Paperback, ISBN: 978-1-58958-560-7
Hardcover, ISBN: 978-1-58958-561-4

**2017 Best International Book Award,
Mormon History Association**

Praise for *The Trek East*:

"In *The Trek East*, Dr. Shinji Takagi has produced a masterful treatment of Mormonism's foundation in Japan. Takagi takes an approach that informs us of Mormonism in Japan in a manner that focuses on inputs and results, environmental conditions in Japan and cultural biases of a Mormonism informed by western assumptions."
— Meg Stout, *The Millennial Star*

"This is a wonderful book, full of historical knowledge on a lesser-known subject in LDS history. The author, who is Japanese, LDS and lives in Virginia, is deeply invested in the subject and carefully includes all sides of the history."
— Mike Whitmer, *Deseret News*

"A monumental work of scholarship. . . . I can't imagine that any future study of this period could hope to provide a more thorough and engrossing analytical study of the origins and growth of the Church in Japan. This remarkable contribution is unlikely ever to be supplanted."
— Van C. Gessel, *Journal of Mormon History*

Joseph Smith's Polygamy: Toward a Better Understanding

Brian C. Hales and Laura H. Hales

Paperback, ISBN: 978-1-58958-723-6

In the last several years a wealth of information has been published on Joseph Smith's practice of polygamy. For some who were already well aware of this aspect of early Mormon history, the availability of new research and discovered documents has been a wellspring of further insight and knowledge into this topic. For others who are learning of Joseph's marriages to other women for the first time, these books and online publications (including the LDS Church's recent Gospel Topics essays on the subject) can be both an information overload and a challenge to one's faith.

In this short volume, Brian C. Hales (author of the 3-volume Joseph Smith's Polygamy set) and Laura H. Hales wade through the murky waters of history to help bring some clarity to this episode of Mormonism's past, examining both the theological explanations of the practice and the accounts of those who experienced it first hand. As this episode of Mormon history involved more than just Joseph and his first wife Emma, this volume also includes short biographies of the 36 women who were married to the Prophet but whose stories of faith, struggle, and courage have been largely forgotten and ignored over time. While we may never fully understand the details and reasons surrounding this practice, Brian and Laura Hales provide readers with an accessible, forthright, and faithful look into this challenging topic so that we can at least come toward a better understanding.

Modern Polygamy and Mormon Fundamentalism: The Generations after the Manifesto

Brian C. Hales

Paperback, ISBN: 978-1-58958-109-8

Winner of the John Whitmer Historical Association's Smith-Pettit Best Book Award

This fascinating study seeks to trace the historical tapestry that is early Mormon polygamy, details the official discontinuation of the practice by the Church, and, for the first time, describes the many zeal-driven organizations that arose in the wake of that decision. Among the polygamous groups discussed are the LeBaronites, whose "blood atonement" killings sent fear throughout Mormon communities in the late seventies and the eighties; the FLDS Church, which made news recently over its construction of a compound and temple in Texas (Warren Jeffs, the leader of that church, is now standing trial on two felony counts after his being profiled on America's Most Wanted resulted in his capture); and the Allred and Kingston groups, two major factions with substantial membership statistics both in and out of the United States. All these fascinating histories, along with those of the smaller independent groups, are examined and explained in a way that all can appreciate.

Praise for *Modern Polygamy and Mormon Fundamentalism*:

"This book is the most thorough and comprehensive study written on the sugbject to date, providing readers with a clear, candid, and broad sweeping overview of the history, teachings, and practices of modern fundamentalist groups."
—Alexander L. Baugh, Associate Professor of Church History and Doctrine, Brigham Young University

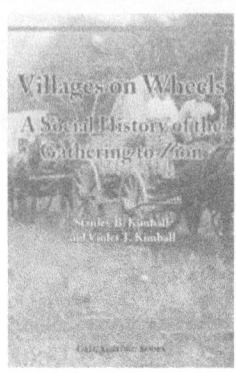

Villages on Wheels: A Social History of the Gathering to Zion

Stanley B. Kimball and Violet T. Kimball

ISBN: 978-1-58958-119-7

The enduring saga of Mormonism is its great trek across the plains, and understanding that trek was the life work of Stanley B. Kimball, master of Mormon trails. This final work, a collaboration he began and which was completed after his death in 2003 by his photographer-writer wife, Violet, explores that movement westward as a social history, with the Mormons moving as "villages on wheels."

Set in the broader context of transcontinental migration to Oregon and California, the Mormon trek spanned twenty-two years, moved approximately 54,700 individuals, many of them in family groups, and left about 7,000 graves at the trailside.

Like a true social history, this fascinating account in fourteen chapters explores both the routines of the trail—cooking, cleaning, laundry, dealing with bodily functions—and the dramatic moments: encountering Indians and stampeding buffalo, giving birth, losing loved ones to death, dealing with rage and injustice, but also offering succor, kindliness, and faith. Religious observances were simultaneously an important part of creating and maintaining group cohesiveness, but working them into the fabric of the grueling day-to-day routine resulted in adaptation, including a "sliding Sabbath." The role played by children and teens receives careful scrutiny; not only did children grow up quickly on the trail, but the gender boundaries guarding their "separate spheres" blurred under the erosion of concentrating on tasks that had to be done regardless of the age or sex of those available to do them. Unexpected attention is given to African Americans who were part of this westering experience, and Violet also gives due credit to the "four-legged heroes" who hauled the wagons westward.

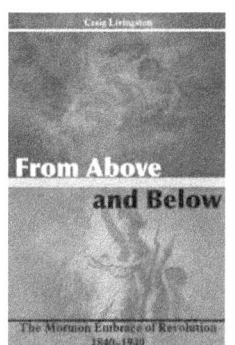

From Above and Below: The Mormon Embrace of Revolution, 1840–1940

Craig Livingston

Paperback, ISBN: 978-1-58958-621-5

2014 Best International Book Award, Mormon History Association

Praise for *From Above and Below*:

"In this engaging study, Craig Livingston examines Mormon responses to political revolutions across the globe from the 1840s to the 1930s. Latter-day Saints saw utopian possibilities in revolutions from the European tumults of 1848 to the Mexican Revolution. Highlighting the often radical anti-capitalist and anti-imperialist rhetoric of Mormon leaders, Livingston demonstrates how Latter-day Saints interpreted revolutions through their unique theology and millennialism."
--Matthew J. Grow, author of *Liberty to the Downtrodden: Thomas L. Kane, Romantic Reformer*

"Craig Livingston's landmark book demonstrates how 21st-century Mormonism's arch-conservatism was preceded by its pro-revolutionary worldview that was dominant from the 1830s to the 1930s. Shown by current opinion-polling to be the most politically conservative religious group in the United States, contemporary Mormons are unaware that leaders of the LDS Church once praised radical liberalism and violent revolutionaries. By this pre-1936 Mormon view, 'The people would reduce privilege and exploitation in the crucible of revolution, then reforge society in a spiritual union of peace' before the Coming of Christ and His Millennium. With profound research in Mormon sources and in academic studies about various social revolutions and political upheavals, Livingston provides a nuanced examination of this little-known dimension of LDS thought which tenuously balanced pro-revolutionary enthusiasms with anti-mob sentiments."
--D. Michael Quinn, author of *Elder Statesman: A Biography of J. Reuben Clark*

A House for the Most High: The Story of the Original Nauvoo Temple

Matthew McBride

Hardcover, ISBN: 978-1-58958-016-9

This awe-inspiring book is a tribute to the perseverance of the human spirit. *A House for the Most High* is a groundbreaking work from beginning to end with its faithful and comprehensive documentation of the Nauvoo Temple's conception. The behind-the-scenes stories of those determined Saints involved in the great struggle to raise the sacred edifice bring a new appreciation to all readers. McBride's painstaking research now gives us access to valuable first-hand accounts that are drawn straight from the newspaper articles, private diaries, journals, and letters of the steadfast participants.

The opening of this volume gives the reader an extraordinary window into the early temple-building labors of the besieged Church of Jesus Christ of Latter-day Saints, the development of what would become temple-related doctrines in the decade prior to the Nauvoo era, and the 1839 advent of the Saints in Illinois. The main body of this fascinating history covers the significant years, starting from 1840, when this temple was first considered, to the temple's early destruction by a devastating natural disaster. A well-thought-out conclusion completes the epic by telling of the repurchase of the temple lot by the Church in 1937, the lot's excavation in 1962, and the grand announcement in 1999 that the temple would indeed be rebuilt. Also included are an astonishing appendix containing rare and fascinating eyewitness descriptions of the temple and a bibliography of all major source materials. Mormons and non-Mormons alike will discover, within the pages of this book, a true sense of wonder and gratitude for a determined people whose sole desire was to build a sacred and holy temple for the worship of their God.

Mormon and Maori

Marjorie Newton

Paperback, ISBN: 978-1-58958-639-0

**2015 Best International Book Award,
Mormon History Association**

Praise for *The Liberal Soul*:

"*Mormon and Maori* is the result of a labor of love that reflects not years but decades of diligent research. Indeed, in combination with Newton's earlier *Tiki and Temple*, it constitutes the most detailed discussion in print of the fascinating 160-year saga of accommodation and adjustment between Maori culture and Mormonism. Unflinchingly honest yet unfailingly compassionate, *Mormon and Maori* is a must-read for anyone interested in the extraordinary history of the LDS experience in New Zealand."
— Grant Underwood, Professor of History, Brigham Young University

"*Mormon and Maori* offers a substantial historical account that structures and organizes *te iwi* Māori's (The Māori people's) often complex relationship and attachment to an American religion. In this respect Newton's work should be considered groundbreaking."
— Gina Colvin, *Journal of Mormon History*

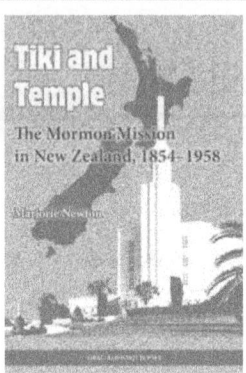

Tiki and Temple: The Mormon Mission in New Zealand, 1854–1958

Marjorie Newton

Paperback, ISBN: 978-1-58958-121-0

**2013 Best International Book Award,
Mormon History Association**

From the arrival of the first Mormon missionaries in New Zealand in 1854 until statehood and the dedication of the Hamilton New Zealand Temple in 1958, Tiki and Temple tells the enthralling story of Mormonism's encounter with the genuinely different but surprisingly harmonious Maori culture.

Mormon interest in the Maori can be documented to 1832, soon after Joseph Smith organized the Church of Jesus Christ of Latter-day Saints in America. Under his successor Brigham Young, Mormon missionaries arrived in New Zealand in 1854, but another three decades passed before they began sustained proselytising among the Maori people—living in Maori pa, eating eels and potatoes with their fingers from communal dishes, learning to speak the language, and establishing schools. They grew to love—and were loved by—their Maori converts, whose numbers mushroomed until by 1898, when the Australasian Mission was divided, the New Zealand Mission was ten times larger than the parent Australian Mission.

The New Zealand Mission of the Mormon Church was virtually two missions—one to the English-speaking immigrants and their descendants, and one to the tangata whenua—"people of the land." The difficulties this dichotomy caused, as both leaders and converts struggled with cultural differences and their isolation from Church headquarters, make a fascinating story. Drawing on hitherto untapped sources, including missionary journals and letters and government documents, this absorbing book is the fullest narrative available of Mormonism's flourishing in New Zealand.

Although written primarily for a Latter-day Saint audience, this book fills a gap for anyone interested in an accurate and coherent account of the growth of Mormonism in New Zealand.

Textual Studies of the Doctrine and Covenants: The Plural Marriage Revelation

William Victor Smith

Paperback, ISBN: 978-1-58958-690-1
Hardcover, ISBN: 978-1-58958-691-8

Joseph Smith's July 12, 1843, revelation on plural marriage was the last of his formal written revelations and a transformational moment in Mormonism. While acting today as the basis for the doctrine of eternal nuclear families, the revelation came forth during a period of theological expansion as Smith was in the midst of introducing new temple rituals, radical doctrines on God and humanity, a restructured priesthood and ecclesiastical hierarchy, and, of course, the practice of plural marriage.

In this volume, author William V. Smith examines the text of this complicated and rough revelation to explore the motivation for its existence, how it reflects this dynamic theology of the Nauvoo period, and how the revelation was utilized and reinterpreted as Mormonism fully embraced and later abandoned polygamy.

Praise for *Textual Studies*:

"No Mormon text is as ritually important and as fundamentally mysterious as Doctrine and Covenants 132. William V. Smith's work is a fine example of what a serious-minded and meticulous blend of source and redaction critical methods can tell us about the revelations produced by Joseph Smith. This is a model of what the future of Mormon scriptural studies should be."
— Stephen C. Taysom, author of *Shakers, Mormons, and Religious Worlds: Conflicting Visions, Contested Boundaries*

Hearken, O Ye People: The Historical Setting of Joseph Smith's Ohio Revelations

Mark Lyman Staker

Hardcover, ISBN: 978-1-58958-113-5

2010 Best Book Award - John Whitmer Historical Association
2011 Best Book Award - Mormon History Association

More of Mormonism's canonized revelations originated in or near Kirtland than any other place. Yet many of the events connected with those revelations and their 1830s historical context have faded over time. Mark Staker reconstructs the cultural experiences by which Kirtland's Latter-day Saints made sense of the revelations Joseph Smith pronounced. This volume rebuilds that exciting decade using clues from numerous archives, privately held records, museum collections, and even the soil where early members planted corn and homes. From this vast array of sources he shapes a detailed narrative of weather, religious backgrounds, dialect differences, race relations, theological discussions, food preparation, frontier violence, astronomical phenomena, and myriad daily customs of nineteenth-century life. The result is a "from the ground up" experience that today's Latter-day Saints can all but walk into and touch.

Praise for *Hearken O Ye People*:

"I am not aware of a more deeply researched and richly contextualized study of any period of Mormon church history than Mark Staker's study of Mormons in Ohio. We learn about everything from the details of Alexander Campbell's views on priesthood authority to the road conditions and weather on the four Lamanite missionaries' journey from New York to Ohio. All the Ohio revelations and even the First Vision are made to pulse with new meaning. This book sets a new standard of in-depth research in Latter-day Saint history."
-Richard Bushman, author of *Joseph Smith: Rough Stone Rolling*

"To be well-informed, any student of Latter-day Saint history and doctrine must now be acquainted with the remarkable research of Mark Staker on the important history of the church in the Kirtland, Ohio, area."
-Neal A. Maxwell Institute, Brigham Young University

For the Cause of Righteousness: A Global History of Blacks and Mormonism, 1830-2013

Russell W. Stevenson

Paperback, ISBN: 978-1-58958-529-4

**2015 Best Book Award,
Mormon History Association**

"In Russell Stevenson's *For the Cause of Righteousness: A Global History of Blacks and Mormonism*, he extends the story of Mormonism's long-standing priesthood ban to the broader history of the Church's interaction with blacks. In so doing he introduces both relevant atmospherics and important new context. These should inform all future discussions of this surprisingly enduring subject."
— Lester E. Bush, author of "Mormonism's Negro Doctrine: An Historical Overview"

"Russell Stevenson has produced a terrific compilation. Invaluable as a historical resource, and as a troubling morality tale. The array of documents compellingly reveals the tragedy and inconsistency of racial attitudes, policies, and doctrines in the LDS tradition, and the need for eternal vigilance in negotiating a faith that must never be unmoored from humaneness."
— Terryl L. Givens, author of *Parley P. Pratt: The Apostle Paul of Mormonism* and *By the Hand of Mormon: The American Scripture that Launched a New World Religion*

"You might wonder what a White man could possibly say to two Black women about Black Mormon history. Surprisingly a whole lot! As people who consider ourselves well informed in African-American Mormon History, we found a wealth of new information in *For the Cause of Righteousness*. Russell Stevenson's well-researched exploration of Blacks and Mormonism is an informative read, not just for those interested in Black history, but American history as well."
— Tamu Smith and Zandra Vranes (a.k.a. Sistas in Zion), authors, *Diary of Two Mad Black Mormons*

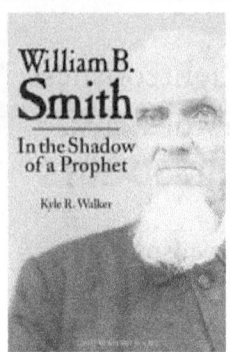

William B. Smith: In the Shadow of a Prophet

Kyle R. Walker

Paperback, ISBN: 978-1-58958-503-4

Younger brother of Joseph Smith, a member of the Quorum of the Twelve Apostles, and Church Patriarch for a time, William Smith had tumultuous yet devoted relationships with Joseph, his fellow members of the Twelve, and the LDS and RLDS (Community of Christ) churches. Walker's imposing biography examines not only William's complex life in detail, but also sheds additional light on the family dynamics of Joseph and Lucy Mack Smith, as well as the turbulent intersections between the LDS and RLDS churches. *William B. Smith: In the Shadow of a Prophet* is a vital contribution to Mormon history in both the LDS and RLDS traditions.

Praise for *William B. Smith*:

"Bullseye! Kyle Walker's biography of Joseph Smith Jr.'s lesser known younger brother William is right on target. It weaves a narrative that is searching, balanced, and comprehensive. Walker puts this former Mormon apostle solidly within a Smith family setting, and he hits the mark for anyone interested in Joseph Smith and his family. Walker's biography will become essential reading on leadership dynamics within Mormonism after Joseph Smith's death." — Mark Staker, author *Hearken, O Ye People: The Historical Setting of Joseph Smith's Ohio Revelations*

"This perceptive biography on William, the last remaining Smith brother, provides a thorough timeline of his life's journey and elucidates how his insatiable discontent eventually tempered the once irascible young man into a seasoned patriarch loved by those who knew him." — Erin B. Metcalfe, president (2014–15) John Whitmer Historical Association

"I suspect that this comprehensive treatment will serve as the definitive biography for years to come; it will certainly be difficult to improve upon." — Joe Steve Swick III, Association for Mormon Letters

www.ingramcontent.com/pod-product-compliance
Lightning Source LLC
Chambersburg PA
CBHW051117160426
43195CB00014B/2246